All About Faith 3

Also by Anne and Niall Boyle

All About Faith 1
All About Faith 2

All About Faith

Book Three
The Moral Challenge

Anne Boyle and Niall Boyle

Gill & Macmillan

Gill & Macmillan Ltd
Hume Avenue
Park West
Dublin 12
with associated companies throughout the world
www.gillmacmillan.ie

© Anne and Niall Boyle 2002

0 7171 3325 7
Illustrations by Karen Allsop
Maps by Design Image
Print origination in Ireland by Carole Lynch
Imprimatur: Most Rev. Michael Smith DCL, Bishop of Meath

The paper used in this book is made from the wood pulp of managed forests. For every tree felled, at least one tree is planted, thereby renewing natural resources.

Photo Acknowledgments
Many thanks to the following for granting permission to reproduce images in this book: Image File; The Art Archive; Robert Harding Pictures; the Bridgeman Photo Library; Frank Spooner Pictures; Mary Evans Picture Library; AKG; Corbis; PA Photos; Scala; the National Gallery, London; the National Gallery, Dublin; Reuters; the *Irish Times*.

Contents

Contents

Part One

Making Moral Decisions

CHAPTER ONE

INTRODUCTION TO MORALITY

Robinson Crusoe

In 1719, Daniel Defoe published a best-selling novel entitled *Robinson Crusoe*. It is a classic tale of adventure and survival against the odds. It tells the story of the sole survivor of a shipwreck, a man named Robinson Crusoe, who finds himself castaway on a remote, uninhabited island, far from the regular shipping routes.

At first Crusoe is in despair at his predicament.

> *I am cast upon a horrible desolate island, without any hope of recovery.*

Slowly, however, with patience and considerable ingenuity, Crusoe not only survives but also gradually transforms this remote island into a tropical paradise.

How is Crusoe able to survive? Fortunately, the island has a freshwater spring and an abundance of wild animals. Further, Crusoe discovers that the sailing vessel on which he had been travelling has run aground on the island's shoreline. From this ship he salvages all the tools and materials he needs to build a fortified home, as well as the seeds to plant crops and the means to make his own clothes.

For the next twenty-four years, Crusoe lives alone on the island. Then, one day, a group of cannibals arrive from a neighbouring island. Crusoe uses the muskets he had recovered from the ship, all those years ago, to drive them off and to rescue one of their victims. Crusoe names this man *Friday*, because that is the day of the week on which he rescues him.

At first, Crusoe treats Friday as his servant. Later, the two men become good friends. Crusoe teaches Friday to speak English and convinces him to become a Christian. Finally, after Crusoe has spent twenty-eight years, two months and nineteen days on the island, he and Friday are rescued. A merchant vessel passes within visual range of the island. It spots their signal fire and sends a shore party to investigate. Crusoe and Friday finally escape the island.

Reflection

When Daniel Defoe wrote *Robinson Crusoe*, he intended to show that any individual human being could achieve almost anything on his/her own. But if one looks carefully at the story, one can see that Defoe *failed* entirely to prove his claim.

Consider the following points:

■ Robinson Crusoe could not have survived without the items he salvaged from the shipwreck. These things (e.g. tools and weapons) were made by *other people*.

■ In the novel, Defoe says that Crusoe found his long years of isolation a terrible ordeal. He was extremely lonely. If Friday had not arrived to provide *friendship*, Crusoe might well have lost the will to live on alone.

■ Without outside help, Crusoe would have been unable to escape from the island and return safely home. *Other people* had to come and rescue him.

The Meaning of Morality

As our reflection on the story of *Robinson Crusoe* has shown, *no one is an island*. People need each other.

We live in complex communities where, on average, we spend two-thirds of each day in the company of others, whether it is working, playing, talking or worshipping together.

Human beings are *social* creatures. This undeniable fact raises a very important question: how should we behave towards one another? This is the question that *morality* seeks to answer. Morality may be defined as *a set of beliefs which offer people guidance about the rightness or wrongness, goodness or badness of human actions.*

QUESTIONS

1. Having considered the story of *Robinson Crusoe*, explain what the poet John Donne meant when he wrote that *No man is an island, entire of itself.*
2. What is *morality*?

Exploring Morality

We shall now turn to explore the different elements of our definition of morality.

■ We will begin with an explanation of what is meant by *human actions*.

■ Then, we will examine how we come to hold certain moral beliefs or *values*.

Human Actions

Human actions can be grouped under two headings:

■ *moral* actions and ■ *non-moral* actions.

To understand the difference between them consider the following examples:

1.	2.
A person accidentally trips and falls down a flight of stairs.	A person jumps into a river to save someone from drowning.
In this case the person does *not* make a choice. This is something that simply *happens* to him/her.	In this case the person *does* make a choice. This is something he/she *decides* to do.
The person is *not* in control here. It is an *accident*.	The person *is* in control here. It is done *deliberately*.
This is a *non-moral action*.	This is a *moral action*.
It is *neither* morally good nor bad.	It is a morally good one.

To summarise:

A moral action is one which is in the control of the person doing it.

Whenever people *know* what they are doing and *freely choose* to do it, then they are in control of their actions. If people are in control of their actions, it follows that they are *responsible* for the consequences of their actions. As a result they can be *blamed* if their actions are bad or *praised* if they are good.

QUESTIONS

1. Explain what is meant by a *moral action*.
2. In each of the following examples, state whether it is a *moral* action or a *non-moral* action.
   (a) A woman who chooses to protest against the construction of a nuclear power plant.
   (b) A man who chooses to drive his car when he suspects that he has consumed alcohol above the legal limit.
   (c) A man who accidentally falls off a ladder while repairing the roof of his house.
   (d) A woman who is late for an important appointment because a national bus and rail strike has cancelled all services at very short notice.
   (e) A man who damages a water pipe while working in an area which he had been assured was safe to dig.
   (f) A woman who goes to visit an elderly relative who has been admitted to hospital.

Socialisation

From the moment of birth, human beings begin learning. At first, people generally learn things from their immediate family. It is in the family that most people take their initial steps in learning how to relate to others, and so learn how to live in a *community*.

The way in which people learn how they should behave in their community is called *socialisation*. As people grow into adulthood, so too does the variety of influences on their *values*.

Values

We may define a *value* as

anything or anyone considered to be good, desirable, important or worthwhile.

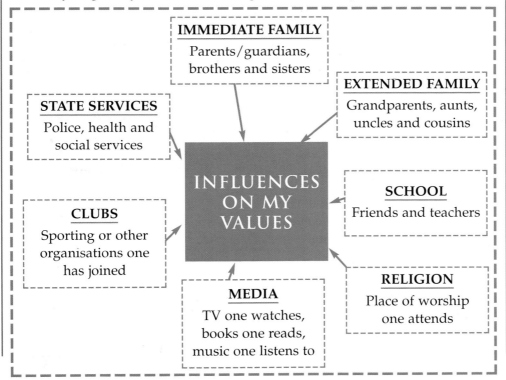

Everyone has values. A singer values her voice and protects it. A sportsman values his fitness and trains to preserve it.

People gradually acquire a set of values as they grow up by:

- Following the *example* set by people they trust.
- Learning from the *consequences* of their own actions and those of others.
- Accepting the *rules* laid down by their family, school, religion and society.

QUESTIONS

1. What is *socialisation*?
2. What is a *value*?
3. How do people acquire a set of values as they grow up?

Friendship

Outside of their own families, the most powerful influence on young people is their circle of friends among their *peers* (i.e. people of the same age group).

Psychologists have long acknowledged the power of one's friends to influence one's values either for good or ill.

Genuine friendships are based on *mutual respect* and a *concern* for what is in each other's *best* interest.

Such friendships can help people to:

- Be more considerate of the needs of others and so encourage them to be more generous and sharing.
- Develop character by giving support and encouragement when facing an important decision.
- Feel wanted and valued, and so build up their self-confidence and self-worth.

QUESTIONS

1. List five qualities that you consider to be the most important in a genuine friendship. In each case explain your choice.

2. There is an old Maori proverb which states:

   One rotten fish plus one fresh fish soon equals two rotten fish.

   What is the point of this proverb in relation to forming friendships with people?

JOURNAL WORK

George Washington once offered this advice:

Be kind to all, but intimate with few, and let those few be well tried before you give them your trust and confidence.

True friendship is a plant of slow growth, and must undergo and withstand the shocks of adversity before it is entitled to the name.

(a) What does Washington mean when he says that people should be *intimate with few and let those few be well tried?*

(b) Why does he describe true friendship as *a plant of slow growth?*

The Role of Values

The values a person holds influences him/her to act in a certain way.

For example, high examination results are a value for some students, because the better the grades they achieve, the greater their job opportunities will be. They will, therefore, do certain things and avoid certain things in order to obtain good results.

When people have to decide what is the right thing to do when faced with a moral choice, their decisions are generally based on the values they hold.

As a person matures, it is hoped that he/she will move away from being pre-occupied with *material values*, such as possessions and wealth, and appreciate the greater importance of *spiritual values*, such as God, love and friendship.

Traditionally, people have accepted one or other of the major world religions as a reliable and trustworthy guide, where spiritual values are concerned.

In the next chapter, we shall examine the role religion can play in helping people to develop good values and make the right decision, when faced with a moral choice.

QUESTIONS

1. In each of the following cases state whether it is a *material value* or a *spiritual value*.

   (a) Giving money to the poor.

   (b) Respecting another person's property.

   (c) Buying only expensive designer label clothing.

   (d) Telling the truth.

   (e) Seeking a promotion and a pay rise.

   (f) Investing in a successful business.

   (g) Comforting a friend in his/her time of need.

2. Consider the following sources of values. In each case state whether it is encouraging the development of good values or bad ones. Explain your answers.

   (a) A *neighbour* who organises a sponsored marathon to raise funds for charity.

   (b) A *student* who encourages his/her classmates to use illegal drugs.

   (c) A *parent* who teaches his/her child to pray.

   (d) A *judge* who sentences a convicted murderer to a life sentence in prison.

   (e) A *team manager* who encourages his players to deliberately injure the star player of a rival team.

   (f) A *T.V. commercial* that aims to convince people to buy expensive cosmetics that do not actually do what they claim.

   (g) A *priest* who encourages his parishioners to become involved in voluntary work to help people in need.

CHAPTER TWO

RELIGION AND MORALITY

Introduction

Each of the major world religions offers detailed guidance as to how people can live good lives and find lasting happiness. In some countries, however, organised religion no longer occupies the central role in people's lives that it once did.

Secularism

Until recently the majority of people in the Western world attended some form of religious service and generally accepted the guidance of their religious leaders on moral issues. Many still do, but a large number do not.

This decline in active membership of an organised religion and the lessening of religion's influence on many people's values is called *secularism*.

QUESTIONS

1. What is meant by *secularism*?
2. Read the following extract by an Irish priest.

    When I was a student in university, around 1960, an amazing scene took place every day in the library at noon: everyone there stood and in silence said the Angelus. Even a Buddhist girl from Thailand, whom I knew quite well, stood in silence. I would love to know when exactly the custom died, but I know that it now would be unthinkable for anyone to make such a public gesture; I wouldn't do it myself. Then, only a brave person would sit down; now only a brave person would stand up. A different outlook is dominant today.

    Adapted from M.P. Gallagher, *Help My Unbelief*

    Having read this extract, what are your reflections on:
    (a) The impact of secularism on contemporary Western society.
    (b) The way in which many people view public displays of religious beliefs today.

JOURNAL WORK

Read the following statement:

The growth of secularism in Western society can be seen in the way Christian festivals such as Christmas have been used as commercial opportunities by big business.

Do you agree/disagree? Explain your answer.

A Complex Situation

While it is true that large numbers of people have fallen away from the practice of religion, studies have also revealed a sharp decline in atheism. It seems that an increasing number of people in Western society are moving into a middle *no-man's land* of confusion regarding questions about God and the meaning of life.

Surveys show that a majority of Western Europeans, for example, continue to believe in God's existence and in life after death. Such beliefs still play a significant role in the lives of many people who do not identify themselves as members of a particular organised religion.

For example, in the Irish context, Christianity has become so much a part of the social fabric that many people who do not attend any religious services often expect to be able to marry in their local church, to have their children christened there and to hold funeral services for deceased relatives there.

Many people who do not identify themselves as either Catholic or Protestant still have a strong sense that these religious ceremonies are the right ways to deal with such important events.

Western European attitudes to religion, and Ireland is no exception here, would appear to mirror other aspects of social and economic life. Many people are not joining a religion, but neither are they joining trade unions nor political parties to the same extent as before.

Our society seems to be going through an era of what the sociologist Grace Davie calls:

Believing but not belonging:

Religion is considered by many people to be a personal, *private* affair. But this is to *misunderstand* the nature of religion. Religion is far *more* than a way of understanding the world. It is also *a way of living in it*.

Christianity has always emphasised the need for people to worship together as a community. Doing this helps to keep a person's faith in God alive by opening out his/her relationship with God to include caring for *other* people.

The current growth of secularism poses a serious challenge to all the major world religions. However, it has led many Christians to take a hard look at the meaning and importance of religion in their lives.

It has encouraged a growing number of people to develop a deeper faith in God, one rooted in a strong personal commitment and demonstrated by their active participation in the religious, social and political life of their community.

In the following chapters we shall examine the ways in which Christians seek to follow Jesus' command to

Love God and love thy neighbour as thyself.
Luke 10:25-27

QUESTIONS

1. State *two* examples of how religion still plays a *significant role* in the lives of people who do not identify themselves as members of a particular organised religion.
2. What does Grace Davie mean when she says that we are living in an era where many people in Western society are *Believing, but not belonging*?
3. Why has Christianity always emphasised the need for people to worship together as a community?

Humanism

Humanists do not consider the growth of secularism to be regrettable. On the contrary, they see it as a positive development. Humanists are either agnostics or atheists. They do *not* believe in God.

Humanist believe that:

■ Morality is a code for living invented entirely by human beings.

■ People can be happy and fulfilled without any religious dimension to their lives.

■ Religion acts as a barrier preventing human progress.

To support this claim they point to the harm done by members of the different world religions throughout history.

Response to Humanism

Jews, Christians and Muslims respond to humanists by stating that:

■ religion is a trustworthy guide to leading a good life;
    and
■ religion is a great force for good in the world.

1 A trustworthy guide

In modern society there are many conflicting opinions on moral issues such as abortion, race relations, tax evasion and so on. How is it possible for people to know what is right and what is wrong?

Consider the following:

■ If, as humanists say, morality is a purely human invention, then it is open to influence by threat of force, opinion polls or simply how the majority of people feel at a particular time.

■ Sincerity is a good and necessary thing in our dealings with people, but it is usually *not* enough in itself. For instance, dictators such as Hitler and Stalin may have been sincere in what they did. The awful things they did, no matter how sincere they were, can *never* be justified or declared good.

Humanists believe that morality should be decided by human reason alone, without any reference to God.

Jews, Christians and Muslims profoundly disagree with humanists. They say that something *more* than human reason is needed to guide people in matters of morality.

In contrast to humanists, they believe that:

■ God exists.

■ God is utterly good.

■ God's plan for living a good life can be found recorded in their sacred scriptures.

■ These holy books contain guidance of enormous depth and wisdom as to what makes life worthwhile and what constitutes a good person.

■ The way to lasting peace and happiness is to be found in faithfully following the teachings of one's religion.

2 A force for good

Jews, Christians and Muslims admit that members of the world's religions have committed terrible deeds while claiming to be 'doing God's work'.

Such evil acts, however, are examples of how unscrupulous and wicked people have *abused* religion to justify their actions and used it as a smokescreen to disguise their *own* selfish purposes.

In contrast to the destructive behaviour of such people, Judaism, Christianity and Islam teach that people should strive to:

■ Love and respect one another.

■ Avoid selfishness in all its forms.

■ Work for justice by protecting the poor, the distressed and all those who are in need.

■ Promote peace and harmony between people.

These religious values have positively influenced countless millions of people over the centuries. Individuals, such as Paul, the Buddha, Muhammad and Mother Teresa of Calcutta, have taught people about the importance of love and forgiveness. They have inspired many people to strive to make the world a better place in which to live.

QUESTIONS

1. What is a *humanist*?
   In your answer explain a humanist's views on:
   - God   ■ religion   ■ morality.
2. Read each of the following statements. Identify those that are *true* and those that are *false*.
   (a) Christians believe that morality should be decided by human reason alone, without reference to God.
   (b) Humanists believe that God is the ultimate source of our standards of what is good and what is evil.
   (c) The holy books of Judaism, Christianity and Islam contain guidance as to what makes life worthwhile and what constitutes a good person.
3. State *two* reasons that Jews, Christians and Muslims give for declaring that religion is a great force for good.

The Unique Authority of Jesus

The Gospels stories show that Jesus Christ understood the needs, the limitations and hopes of human beings. Christians claim that the world's many problems would be more readily solved if people followed his example and allowed the message he preached to guide them.

Consider the founders of Buddhism and Islam. Buddhists believe that the Buddha was *the enlightened one*. Muslims believe that Muhammad was *the prophet of Allah*.

Both the Buddha and Muhammad taught many profound truths about life. However, neither of them claimed to be divine.

In contrast, Christians believe that Jesus of Nazareth is *God made man*.

Some people today claim that Jesus was a great moral teacher but *not* God.

The Christian writer C.S. Lewis defended Christian belief against this claim. He wrote as follows:

I am trying to prevent anyone saying the really foolish thing that people often say about Jesus: 'I am ready to accept Jesus as a great moral teacher, but I do not accept his claim to be God.' This is the one thing we must not say. A man who was merely a man and said the sort of things Jesus said would not be a great moral teacher. He would either be a lunatic – on the level with the man who says he is a poached egg – or else he would be the devil of hell. You must make your choice. Either this man was, and is, the son of God; or else a madman, or something worse. You can shut him up for a fool, you can spit at him and kill him as a demon; you can fall at his feet and call him Lord and God. But let us not come with any patronising nonsense about his being a great human teacher. He has not left that open to us. He did not intend to.

Christians believe that Jesus is the only Son of God and the second person of the Blessed Trinity. He is *the Way, the Truth and the Life (John 14:6).*

For this reason, Christians believe that the moral teaching of Jesus has a unique authority over that of the other world religions.

QUESTIONS

1. What point is C. S. Lewis making about the identity of Jesus?
2. Why do Christians believe that the moral teaching of Jesus has a unique authority over that of other religions?

THE TEACHING CHRIST
(Moscow School – sixteenth century

This is the icon of Jesus, God and man. The belief that Jesus is divine is suggested by the gold and blue colours.

Notice, the gold background, the golden border of his robe, the golden light in his face, the deep blue of his outer cloak.

The humanity of Jesus is suggested by the brown earthy colour of the inner garment. His hand, in a praying position, perhaps indicating his two natures, points to 'The Book' and 'The Prayer': 'He who follows me will have the light of life.'

CHAPTER THREE

LOVE ONE ANOTHER

Introduction

Once, during a discussion with another Jewish rabbi, Jesus was asked this question:

Which of the Commandments is the most important of all?

Jesus gave this reply:

The most important one is this: You shall love the Lord your God with all your heart, with all your soul, with all your mind and all your strength.
This is the second: You shall love your neighbour as yourself.
Mark 12:29-31

The central message of Jesus can be summarised in one sentence, namely, *Love God and love your neighbour*. Love is the very basis of Christian morality.

Jesus and the Blind Man by Duccio

The Ten Commandments

The Ten Commandments are as follows:

1. I, the Lord, am your God; you shall have no other gods besides me.
2. You shall not take the name of the Lord your God in vain.
3. Remember to keep holy the Sabbath day.
4. Honour your father and your mother.
5. You shall not commit murder.
6. You shall not commit adultery.
7. You shall not steal.
8. You shall not bear false witness against your neighbour.
9. You shall not covet your neighbour's wife.
10. You shall not covet anything that belongs to your neighbour.

Genuine love of God is spelt out in the first three of the Ten Commandments. It means making sure that God is the most important thing for people in every aspect of their lives.

This is not possible, however, without keeping the other seven commandments, which say that people must love and respect one another.

> *He who does not love his brother or sister, whom he has seen,*
> *cannot love God whom he has not seen.*
> 1 John 4:20

The Gospels show that Jesus did not simply speak beautiful words; he *lived by them*. He lived and breathed the spirit of God's commandments. Jesus led by example. When Jesus told his followers that the heart of his message was to *love God and love your neighbour as yourself*, they could see that he did not want them to 'do as I say', but rather *do as I do*!

QUESTIONS

1. Which of the Ten commandments centre on our relationship with God?
2. Which commandments centre on relationships between ourselves and other people and vice versa?

JOURNAL WORK

What do you think is the importance of the Ten Commandments for people today?

The Meaning of Love

The word *love* means different things to different people. The Christian understanding of love, however, can be found in the *New Testament*.

The earliest *New Testament* manuscripts were written in Greek. Unlike English, Greek had more than one word for love. This helped Christian writers to identify *four* different kinds of love.

The four different kinds of love are:

- *Storgé* (pronounced stor-gay)
  This is a warm, general affection or fondness for a thing (e.g. a favourite sport) or a place (e.g. the area in which a person grew up).

- *Eros* (pronounced ear-ros)
  This is a physical attraction to and strong romantic desire for a member of the opposite sex.

- *Philia* (pronounced filly-ah)
  This is a strong, intimate love for and loyalty to close family and friends.

- *Agapé* (pronounced aga-pay)
  This is unconditional love for other people, not just those who love you and are close to you.

The great campaigner for civil rights, Dr Martin Luther King, explained the meaning and importance of agapé in the following way:

> *Agapé is more than romantic love, it is more than friendship. Agapé is understanding, creative, redemptive goodwill to all people. Agapé is an overflowing love that seeks nothing in return. Theologians [i.e. religious thinkers] would say that it is the love of God operating in the human heart. When you rise to love on this level, you love all people, not because you like them, not because their ways appeal to you, but you love them because God loves them. This is what Jesus meant when He said, 'Love your enemies'. And we're glad that He didn't say, 'Like your enemies,' because there are some people that we find it very difficult to like. Liking is an affectionate emotion, and we can't like anyone who would bomb our home. We can't like anyone who would exploit us. We can't like anyone who tramples over us with injustices. We can't like them. But Jesus reminds us that love is greater than liking. Love is understanding, creative, redemptive goodwill towards all people.*

If you really love someone, then you must try to act in their best interest and help them without expectation of personal gain.

QUESTIONS

1. Match the explanation in column *B* with the word in column *A*.

A	B
Storgé	A strong, intimate love for and loyalty to close family and friends.
Eros	An unconditional love for other people, not just those who love you and are close to you.
Philia	A physical attraction to and strong romantic desire for a member of the opposite sex.
Agapé	A warm general affection or fondness for a thing or a place.

2. Read the extract by Dr Martin Luther King once more.
   (a) Explain the difference between *liking* and *loving*.
   (b) No one would like to be assaulted or robbed. How might a Christian *love* someone who had done this to him/her?

Love and Sex

As young people grow and mature into adulthood, interest develops into the relationship between love and sex.

■ The word *sex* is usually understood as the physical act of sexual intercourse (see the section *Human Reproduction*).

■ The word *love*, however, is used to refer to the *entire* personal relationship between a man and a woman, which *includes* their sexual relations.

Developing a Loving Relationship

There are five stages in the development of a loving relationship.

1 Attraction

You are attracted to someone. If the attraction is strong, you will try to meet and get to know that person.

2 Acquaintance

Once you become better acquainted with someone, the attraction may fade away quickly. But if the acquaintance continues, the attraction may grow and friendship blossom.

3 Friendship

Becoming good friends is a special time. You may begin to see the other person in a very romantic, idealistic way. You may see him or her as 'the perfect person' – the only one for you.

4 Affection

At this stage, a real caring or affection develops between a man and a woman. This true affection is based on recognising and accepting each other's limitations, while still caring deeply about that other person.

5 Love

Real love between a man and a woman is a growing thing. It is part of a process.

Paul described this love as

> *always patient and kind; it is never jealous; love is never boastful or conceited; it is never rude or selfish; it does not take offence and is not resentful. Love takes no pleasure in other people's sins but delights in the truth; it is always ready to forgive, to trust, to hope and to endure whatever comes. Love does not come to an end.*
> 1 Corinthians 13:4-8

Real love is concerned with the *inner* person, not just appearances. It means caring about the other person as much as oneself. It means working for the other person's welfare and happiness, rather than using him/her as a means of selfishly satisfying one's own needs or desires.

There is *no shortcut* to the development of a truly loving relationship between a man and a woman. You *cannot* reach the fifth stage of the process without growing through the other four stages.

QUESTIONS

1. What are the qualities that you would find attractive in a member of the opposite sex?

2. (a) What factors cause the initial attraction to sometimes fade away quickly?

    (b) What factors cause the initial attraction to sometimes develop into friendship?

3. The third stage in the development of a loving relationship is sometimes called the 'starry-eyed' phase. It is a wonderful time to experience, but if people get married without having developed their relationship beyond this stage, what kind of problems can it cause after they are married to each other?

4. Read the fifth stage once more. Do you think that it is possible to fall in love at first sight? Give reasons for your answer.

Human Reproduction*

Human reproduction occurs when a male sex cell (the sperm) fertilises a female sex cell (the ovum) after sexual intercourse.

Sexual intercourse is seen by Christians as the highest-form of lovemaking. It is where a man and a woman make a total commitment to each other in a married relationship.

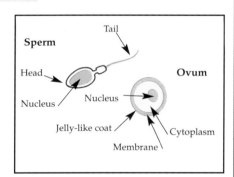

MALE REPRODUCTIVE ORGANS

Penis organ through which sperm are ejected. Becomes erect and stiff during sexual excitement.

Scrotum sac, hanging outside the body, in which testes are kept cool at the ideal temperature for sperm production.

Testes place where sperm are made once puberty is reached.

Seminal vesicle prostate gland These secrete fluids which keep sperm alive. Sperm and fluids together are called **semen**.

*Urethra** carries sperm out of the body.

Sperm duct carries sperm from testes to urethra and penis.

Epididymis coiled tube where sperm are stored.

Foreskin protective covering of glans.

Glans very sensitive tip of penis.

FEMALE REPRODUCTIVE ORGANS

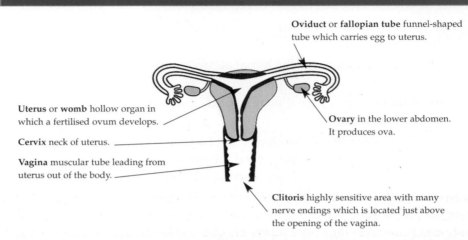

Oviduct or **fallopian tube** funnel-shaped tube which carries egg to uterus.

Uterus or **womb** hollow organ in which a fertilised ovum develops.

Cervix neck of uterus.

Vagina muscular tube leading from uterus out of the body.

Ovary in the lower abdomen. It produces ova.

Clitoris highly sensitive area with many nerve endings which is located just above the opening of the vagina.

SEXUAL INTERCOURSE

Fertilisation takes place within the woman's body when a sperm meets an ovum in the oviduct. Sperm enter the female during **sexual intercourse** when an erect penis is inserted into the vagina. Movement of the pelvis stimulates nerve endings in the penis. This sets off a *reflex action* which results in semen being ejected into the vagina. This is called **ejaculation. Orgasm** is the name given to the intense experience of excitement and pleasure which occurs at the climax of sexual intercourse.

FERTILISATION

Sperm swim from the vagina to the oviducts. If they meet an ovum, fertilisation can take place. One sperm head penetrates the ovum and the two nuclei fuse. This forms a *zygote*, the first cell of a new baby.

The zygote travels to the uterus and becomes implanted in the uterus wall. After this happens it is called an **embryo**. The uterus has prepared for implantation by building up a thick lining, rich in blood vessels.

CONCEPTION

Conception includes fertilisation and the implantation of an embryo in the uterus.

PREGNANCY

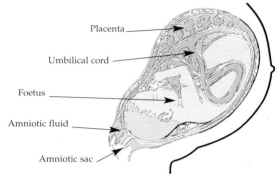

A baby about to be born

Placenta

Umbilical cord

Foetus

Amniotic fluid

Amniotic sac

The time between implantation and birth is called **pregnancy**, or **gestation**. In humans it lasts about thirty-eight weeks. The growing embryo, also called the foetus, becomes surrounded by an **amniotic sac**; i.e. a bag containing watery liquid called **amniotic fluid**. This protects the embryo from knocks.

The embryo needs food and oxygen in order to grow. At first these come directly from the blood vessels in the uterus wall. After a few weeks, however, a special plate-shaped organ develops, called the **placenta**. The baby is connected to the placenta by a cord, called the **umbilical cord**. The foetus receives food and oxygen from the mother's blood, and releases carbon dioxide and other waste matter into it.

During the last few days of pregnancy, the baby moves so that its head is near the cervix. Finally the baby is squeezed out through the vagina by strong contractions of the muscles in the uterus. This is called **labour**.

> * Information adapted from R. Treays, *Essential Biology*

Catholic Teaching

In the *Old Testament* account of the Creation it is written:

> *Male and female God created them. And God blessed them, and God said to them, 'Be fruitful and multiply ....'*
> *Genesis* 1:27-28

It is repeatedly stated that God looked upon his creation and said that *it was good*. As a result, the Catholic Church teaches that:

■ Sex is a *gift* from God that should be used in a loving and respectful way, as through the sexual act a man and a woman express their total love for and commitment to each other.

- Sex can create new life and so concerns more than just the man and woman involved, bringing with it responsibility for *another* human life.
- Sex is the language of *love*, *commitment* and *responsibility*, because in it a man and a woman tell each other that the other is the 'one and only love'. As a result, sex can only find its true expression within a *married* relationship, i.e. where two people commit themselves to one another.
- Sex outside of marriage is an act of deception, because those involved are *not* deliberately and unreservedly committing themselves to love and care for each other, both now, and for all the years to follow.

QUESTIONS

1. Explain the following statement:

   Sex is the language of love, commitment and responsibility.

2. Why does the Catholic Church teach that sex outside of marriage is *an act of deception*?

JOURNAL WORK

Read the following extract written by a married man on the value of *waiting* until one is married before having sexual intercourse.

My wife and I waited until we were married to have sex, which was a different decision than many people nowadays make. But I think it was a good one. Maybe if we'd had sex with other people or with each other before we were married, we'd have been more experienced or knowledgeable. But learning about sex together ... made it that much more special. Also, we didn't have to worry if either of us was 'as good' as the other lovers either of us might have had before....

By being willing to wait until we were married, I felt it was showing my wife that it wasn't just sex that I wanted from her but real, true love and lifelong commitment. And she was showing me the same thing. We really trusted each other.

Adapted from J. Ahlers, *Growing in Christian Morality*

What does the author identify as the benefits to a couple's relationship if they wait until *after* marrying before having sex?

The Meaning of Marriage

A couple busily planning their wedding often find that, absorbed in the exciting and hectic preparations for their big day, it is easy to lose sight of what this event *really* means.

Some people think that the words *marriage* and *wedding* mean exactly the same thing. They do *not*.

- A *wedding* is the *ceremony* in which a couple are married on a *particular* day.
- A *marriage* means *more* than this.
- A *marriage* is the *relationship* that a couple *begin* on their wedding day.

The *rite of marriage* (i.e. ceremony) in the Catholic Church usually takes place as part of the Mass. Before witnesses and in the presence of the priest, the bride and groom begin by answering in turn a series of questions:

- *Have you come to give yourself to each other, freely and without reservation?*
- *Will you love and honour each other for life?*
- *Will you accept children lovingly from God?*

The couple publicly declare that they *understand* what it is they are doing and that they are *freely consenting* to marriage.

Then, the bride and groom exchange *vows* (i.e. make solemn promises to one another). In turn, each says:

> *I take you as my husband/wife, for better or for worse, for richer or for poorer, in sickness and in health, 'til death do us part.*

It is essential that the priest is present in the Catholic marriage ceremony. He represents the Church and accepts the *mutual consent* (i.e. agreement) of the bride and groom. He says to the couple:

> *What God has joined together let no one pull asunder.*

It is not the couple who have joined themselves in marriage but *God* who has made their union complete. This is why the Catholic Church regards marriage as a *sacrament*.

Next, the priest blesses the wedding rings, and each partner in turn places a ring on the third finger of the other's left hand and says:

> *Wear this ring as a sign of our love and fidelity. In the name of the Father, and of the Son, and of the Holy Spirit.*

The endless circle of the wedding ring *symbolises* (i.e. stands for) the couple's commitment to love one another in a relationship that is *permanent* (i.e. life-long) and *exclusive* (i.e. admitting no other partners).

The priest ends by blessing the couple, emphasising how they must be loving and faithful in all the days ahead.

QUESTIONS

1. What is the difference between a *marriage* and a *wedding*?
2. State the three questions the couple are asked by the priest. Why are they asked such questions?
3. What does it mean for the couple to *exchange vows*?
4. Why does the Catholic Church regard marriage as a *sacrament*?
5. What does the *wedding ring* symbolise?

Why Marry?

Traditionally marriage has been considered a good thing because it was accepted as providing the ideal context in which people could:

■ Freely commit themselves to love and care for each other for the rest of their lives.

■ Bring up children in what should be a secure and loving home.

■ Direct the sex instinct towards the most constructive purpose, i.e. to show mutual love and build a happy home.

■ Give and receive companionship and love both in good times and in bad.

Making Marriage Work

In the *Old Testament* account of the Creation it is written

> *A man leaves his father and mother*
> *and is united with his wife,*
> *and they become one.*
> Genesis 2:24

This was written to show that marriage is part of God's plan for human beings. It sets a high standard for marriage: the relationship which a husband and wife should seek to build is to be so close that these two people *become one*.

God's love should be reflected in the love a husband and wife have for each other. For a couple to achieve this and for their marriage to succeed, both husband and wife must continually work at their relationship.

According to experienced marriage counsellors, *both* partners must show:

- genuine commitment;
- willingness to talk to each other;
- close friendship;
- respect for each other's privacy;
- shared basic values;
- readiness to put their relationship ahead of everything else;
- sensitivity in settling disputes;
- willingness to seek and offer forgiveness;
- consideration towards each other in practical ways;
- realistic expectations regarding sex.

It is important to remember that *most marriages succeed*, even though they have to face many pressures and challenges today.

It is advisable for couples intending to marry to attend marriage preparation courses. It is important for a couple to know if they have what it takes to sustain a loving relationship.

Guidance counsellors state that for a marriage to succeed, *both* partners must:

- appreciate and understand the kind of pressures they will have to face, e.g. money, housing, work
  and
- be prepared to support each other through whatever crisis they may face, e.g. illness, bereavement.

QUESTIONS

1. It is recommended that when people wish to marry, they should only do so *with their eyes open*. What does this mean?

2. Why is it advisable for couples intending to marry to attend marriage preparation courses?

CHAPTER FOUR

BEING A DISCIPLE

Introduction

Read any interview with a person who is deeply committed to working with the disabled, fund-raising for orphans, caring for the elderly or campaigning to preserve the environment. All of them have the same thing in common: they all share a deep conviction that this is work they were meant to do. They all have a sense of being somehow *called* to do this work.

Vocation

This sense of being called to do something important in life is referred to as *a vocation*, from the Latin work *vocare* meaning *to call*.

The Conversion of St Paul by Michelangelo

Christians believe that each person is called by God to fulfil his/her own particular vocation in life.

In the Catholic Church people have a choice of *three* ways in which to fulfil their vocation.

This may be as:

- A single or married lay person.

- A monk or nun in a religious community.

- A priest or a bishop.

Each vocation has an important role to play.

It is important to note that no vocation is regarded as more important than another. As Paul wrote to the early Christians:

> *There is as variety of gifts but always the same Holy Spirit; there are all sorts of service to be done, but always the same Lord; working in all sorts of different ways in different people, it is the same God who is working in all of them. The particular way in which the Holy Spirit is given to each person is for a good purpose.*
> *1 Corinthians 12:4-7*

Bishops, priests, religious and laity are all members of the *one family* of God. All are called to be *disciples* of Jesus in today's world.

◄ *St Paul's Sermon in Ephesus*
by Le Seuer

Discipleship

Jesus told his first small band of followers that to be his disciple meant not merely learning his teachings, but also following his example. His disciples were called to be

> *the light of the world.*
> *Matthew* 5:14

Their lives must shine like a beacon of goodness drawing other people to God.

This is just as true for Christians today. When people are baptised and confirmed, they are anointed to *share* in the work of Jesus himself. They are called to confront prejudice and intolerance, to comfort the lonely, to care for the neglected.

Jesus calls on his disciples to live according to very high standards.

> *You must be perfect, as your heavenly father is perfect.*
> *Matthew* 5:48

> *Love your enemies. Do good to those who hate you.*
> *Luke* 6:27

Indeed, the challenge Jesus offers is so demanding that few people, either now or in times past, have been able to follow his teachings completely.

Jesus' teaching sets forth an *ideal*, i.e. a high standard which people should strive to achieve. He understood how difficult people find it to live his way. He acknowledged that

> *The spirit indeed is willing, but the flesh is weak.*
> *Matthew* 28:41

To live as Jesus lived makes enormous demands. It requires great faith, courage and willingness to sacrifice one's own life.

QUESTIONS

1. What is the meaning of the word *vocation*?
2. What did Jesus mean when he called his disciples to be *the light of the world*?
3. Explain the following statement:

   Jesus' teaching sets forth an ideal.

Profile: Mother Teresa, A Vocation to Care for the Poorest of the Poor

When Mother Teresa came to London she found people dying in the streets, and even in their own homes, unloved. 'Here you have a different kind of poverty in the Western world' she said, 'a poverty of spirit, of loneliness, and that is the worst disease in the world today, worse than tuberculosis or leprosy. We have to love.'

This extraordinary woman was born in 1910 in Skopje, Yugoslavia, of Albanian parents. She trained for a year with the Mercy Sisters in Rathfarnham, Dublin. Then, she was sent to teach geography in a school for high-caste Indian girls in Calcutta and eventually became its principal. Gradually, though, she became aware of another vocation within her. She believed that God was calling her to serve him in the poorest of the poor.

She always remembered 10 September 1946 as her 'Day of Decision'. It was then that she asked permission from her religious superiors to work in the slums of Calcutta.

When permission was granted she went first to Patna for intensive nursing training, returning to Calcutta at the end of 1948. She was given permission to open her first slum school and the following year a Bengali girl joined her to form the nucleus of a new order, the Missionaries of Charity. These sisters in their white saris edged with blue stripes were soon to became a familiar sight not only in Calcutta but also in slums throughout the world – Venezuela, Ceylon, Tanzania, Rome, Australia and in London too. Their work today is done with an unforced joy and enthusiasm which are a perfect expression of Christian love – *agapé*.

Mother Teresa did not want people to focus on her own life. The work she did was Christ's work, serving him in the poorest of the poor and the circumstances of her own life were unimportant.

Look again at the parable of the sheep and the goats (*Matthew* 25:31-46). It was often quoted by Mother Teresa and was the basis of her own understanding of her work. As she tended to the dying, cared for lepers, rescued newborn babies from dustbins, she was seeing Christ in the outcast. Her love for them was God's love, flowing through her.

She never worried about money; when needed it seemed to arrive. Mother Teresa saw this as God providing for her own work. When the Pope visited India he gave her the white limousine he had used in his travels. She raffled it and made enough money to start a leper colony. She won many international awards for her work including the Nobel Peace Prize. All prize money went into projects to help people.

She was perhaps best known for her care of the dying. This work started when she picked up a woman from the street who was being eaten alive by rats and ants and the hospitals refused to take her in. Places could only be spared for those with hope of recovery. So she asked the city authorities to provide her with a building where she could take such people. They offered her a disused Hindu temple, which she gratefully accepted. Today it is perhaps the best known home for the dying in the world. Many thousands have been taken there to die in peace, surrounded by love. All must first have been turned away from hospitals.

Mother Teresa never lost her love of teaching. She started a school in the Calcutta slums. They had no building so they met in a compound belonging to a slum family. On the first day she had five pupils. Now the sisters have over 500. Children are taught to read and are given lessons in elementary hygiene – a far cry from teaching geography to middle-class girls.

Work among lepers has also grown from the five who first came to the sisters in 1957 to the many thousands they care for today. If the disease is diagnosed early it can be cured in less than two years. The sisters run a rehabilitation centre to help those who have been cured and offer loving care to those where the disease has gone beyond such help.

In the early days people were sometimes patronising about this woman who went off to serve the poor in the slums. What difference could such a tiny drop in the ocean make to the problems of world poverty? She, herself, pointed out that the ocean would be smaller without that drop. Eventually even the hard-bitten came to recognise her great influence for good. For Christians caught up in the confusions of life in the twenty-first century, Mother Teresa stands out as a reassuring example of the truth of the gospel.

When she died in 1997, her passing was mourned by countless millions. They saw in her life what can be achieved when Christ is taken at his word and followed in simplicity.

Adapted from Diana Morgan, *Christian Perspectives on Contemporary Issues*

QUESTIONS

1. What were the kinds of poverty Mother Teresa identified in a busy Western city like London?
2. When and where was she born?
3. Why did Mother Teresa decide to ask for permission to work in the slums of Calcutta?
4. Name the religious order she founded.
5. Identify the kinds of people whom she helped.
6. Which international award did she win?
7. Why did she become involved in caring for the dying?
8. Describe the work of her rehabilitation centre for victims of leprosy.
9. (a) Why were people sometimes patronising about Mother Teresa's work?
   (b) How did she respond to them?
10. When did Mother Teresa die?

Saints

Throughout the history of the Christian religion there have been many extraordinary men and women who so devoted their lives to doing good and leading others to God, that they have been declared *saints*.

A Christian can only be considered worthy of being declared a saint *after* his/her death. Then a special commission is appointed by the Pope to investigate whether or not the person was, indeed, a saint. The final decision is made by the Pope. This decision to honour a person with the title of saint is called *canonisation*.

QUESTIONS

1. What is a *saint*?
2. Describe the process by which a person is declared a saint.
3. What is *canonisation*?

Entrance to Auschwitz concentration camp

Profile: Maximilian Kolbé, the Saint of Auschwitz

In July 1941 three prisoners escaped from the Nazi concentration camp of Auschwitz. In reprisal, the Nazis picked ten prisoners who would be deliberately starved to death. One of the men was Franciszek Gajowniczek. When he realised his fate he cried out, 'My wife, my children, I shall never see them again.' It was then that the unexpected happened. From the ranks of watching inmates, prisoner 16670 stepped out and offered himself to take this man's place. Then the volunteer was taken with the other nine condemned men to the dreaded bunker, an airless underground cell, to die slowly without food or water.

Prisoner 16670 was a Polish Catholic priest named Maximilian Kolbé. He was forty-seven years old. Before the war he had founded one of the largest monasteries in the world. He had also travelled as a missionary to the Far East. In 1939 he began helping Jewish refugees.

However, in 1941 Father Kolbé was arrested by the Nazis and sent to prison in Warsaw and then deported to Auschwitz. Auschwitz was a terrible place. Human beings were treated in the most inhuman ways imaginable. Thousands died every day from beatings, floggings, torture, disease, starvation and in the gas chambers. Father Kolbé dedicated his life in Auschwitz to helping his fellow prisoners. He would console them, share his food with them, and organise secret church services. He tried to show others, by his own example, that even in such a hellish place God still loved and cared for them.

An eyewitness of those last terrible days of Father Kolbé's life tells us what happened.

'In the cell of the poor wretches there were daily prayers, and hymn singing, in which prisoners from neighbouring cells also joined. When no SS men were in the block I went to the bunker to talk to the men and comfort them. Fervent prayers and songs resounded in all the corridors of the bunker. I had the impression I was in a church. Father Kolbé was leading and the prisoners responded in unison. They were often so deep in prayer that they did not hear that inspecting SS men had descended to the bunker; and the voices fell silent only at the loud yelling of their visitors. When the cells were opened the poor wretches cried loudly and begged for a piece of bread and for water, which they did not receive. If any of the stronger ones approached the door he was immediately kicked in the stomach by the SS men, so that falling backwards on the cement floor he was instantly killed; or he was shot to death ... Father Kolbé bore up bravely; he did not beg and did not complain but raised the spirits of the others ...

Since they had grown very weak, prayers were now only whispered. At every inspection, when almost all the others were now lying on the floor, Father Kolbé was seen kneeling or standing in the centre as he looked cheerfully in the face of the SS men. Two weeks passed in this way. Meanwhile one after another they died, until only Father Kolbé was left. This the authorities felt was too long; the cell was needed for new victims. So one day they brought in the head of the sick quarters, a German, a common criminal named Bock who gave Father Kolbé an injection of carbolic acid in the vein of his left arm. Father Kolbé, with a prayer on his lips, himself gave his arm to the executioner. Unable to watch this I left under the pretext of work to be done. Immediately after the SS men with the executioner left I returned to the cell, where I found Father Kolbé leaning in a sitting position against the back wall with his eyes open and his head drooping sideways. His face was calm and radiant.'

In 1982 the Catholic Church declared Maximilian Kolbé a saint.

Source: Catholic Truth Society

QUESTIONS

1. Who was Maximilian Kolbé?
2. What was Auschwitz?
3. Why did Maximilian Kolbé volunteer to take the place of a fellow prisoner in the death cell?
4. How did Maximilian Kolbé die?

CHAPTER FIVE

BUILDING COMMUNITY

The Importance of Community

Human beings are social creatures. Generally speaking, people want to live in *community*, i.e. to share their lives with others. The need to *belong* is very strong in human beings. This is because being rooted in a family and in a local community helps people to grow in confidence about their individual identities. It helps them to know who they are and where they have come from.

Through friendship, people can be encouraged to be generous, trusting and self-confident. Every person needs to feel wanted and valued by others. Andrew Lascaris has written:

An analysis of suicide rates indicates that life becomes meaningless without positive relationships with other people, without friendship.

Going on holidays by oneself without even the possibility of talking about it with someone else later is no fun at all. Cleaning out one's house and feeding oneself properly, if nobody is ever going to visit you, somehow does not seem to make sense.

Things only happen – become real, alive – when people are together.

Mother Teresa of Calcutta once described *loneliness* as *the greatest disease afflicting Western society*. She called on people to reflect on the true meaning of community. She gave the following example to illustrate how people can be friends to one another.

Some weeks back I heard that there was a Hindu family that had not eaten for some days so I took some rice and I went to the family. Before I knew where I was, the mother of the family had divided the rice into two and she gave the other half to her next door neighbours, who happened to be a Muslim family. Then I asked her, 'How much will all of you have to share? There are ten of you with that bit of rice to share among you.' The mother replied, 'They have not eaten either.' This is greatness.

QUESTIONS

1. What is the meaning of the word *community*?
2. Why is the need to *belong* very strong in human beings?
3. Why is *friendship* so important?
4. What did Mother Teresa once describe as *the greatest disease afflicting Western society*?
5. What is the central message of her story of the Hindu mother's generosity?

Being a Witness

All Christians are called to be *witnesses*, i.e. to publicly give evidence of their love for God and for other people in their community by the way they live their lives. Christians are called to *be* like Jesus in today's world.

I Am Living Among You

The famous Russian author, Leo Tolstoy, tells a story about a poor shoemaker, Martin Avdyeeich. Just a few years after his marriage Martin's wife and young son died. Their deaths left him broken-hearted and empty. Life had no meaning for him. He called into question all that he had known about God, all that he believed about Christ. Where, he asked, was God in his suffering? Was there no consolation for him, no hope? Gradually Martin found peace and comfort in the Bible. How God's people suffered! Yet he saw that there was meaning and purpose in life. God is always near at hand: Christ does care.

One night Martin's eyes grew heavy and his head drooped over the fading print of his Bible. Laying his head down on the open book, he fell into a deep sleep. When he woke the next morning, his heart was filled with expectation and a strange joy. Could it be, or was he only dreaming, that this very day Jesus would visit him? The experience was more than a fanciful dream to Martin. He was certain Christ did speak to him during the night. This day he would have the Lord Jesus with him.

All day long Martin sat at the shop window distracted. He could not work. He searched every face that passed by along the busy street outside. He knew those faces: the old, the young, the tradesmen with whom he had done business, the soldiers, the servants of the well-to-do. Then there were the others, those who just walked the street day after day.

The Russian winter is bitterly cold and from autumn to spring the ground is covered with snow. As Martin sat looking out of his window, he noticed an old soldier. Having shovelled snow for hours, the man was at the point of exhaustion, weary and pierced with the cold. Martin took the soldier in, gave him some hot tea and then talked to him. The old man was lonely and unhappy. Martin consoled him.

Walking in the snow-packed street later in the day, Martin was startled by what he saw. There out in the open near his shop sat a starving woman and her nearly frozen child. Martin ran to help them. During the afternoon Martin noticed that a young boy was in trouble. He had stolen an apple and an old woman was dragging him off to be arrested. Martin intervened on the boy's behalf and the woman forgave the youth. It was a busy day, a disappointing day. That evening Martin sat down and stared emptily into space. He had been so certain that this was the day he would have a visit from Christ and the day was nearly over. He sighed and taking up the book began to read the Gospels. It was still and quiet in the shop. The light was low. Martin felt strangely warm. Suddenly he leaned forward attentively. Had he heard a voice whispering 'Martin, don't you know me?' The old soldier was standing before him! Then the woman with the child in her arms! The boy who had stolen the apple and the woman who had wanted him arrested, suddenly, they too seemed to appear. The moment lingered, then Martin's eyes went down to the pages of the Gospel. He began to read from where he had left off the previous night. 'I was hungry and you gave me to eat; I was thirsty and you gave me to drink; I was a stranger and you took me into your home.' Martin's heart leaped for joy as he came to the bottom of the page. 'In as much as you did this to one of these, you did it to me' (Matthew 25:40).

Christians are called to see Christ in all those whom they meet. They are expected to be friends, not only to their own family members and those who love them, but also to those whom they encounter in school and in the work place.

Christians are expected to give both time and money to support worthy causes. They must take on an active role in community groups. In particular, they must be willing to offer the hand of friendship to those who are lonely, despairing and abandoned. They must demonstrate their belief that each person has an infinite worth in God's eyes. *They are called to be a friend in need.*

Caring for all

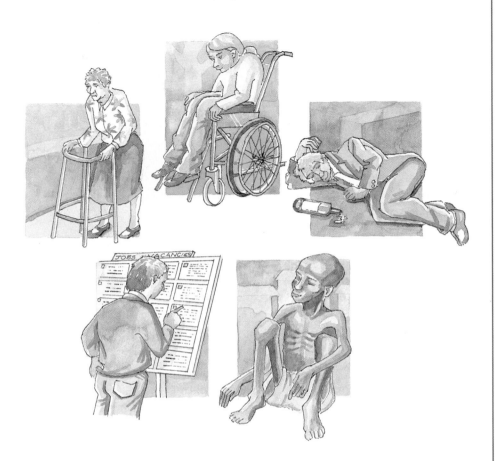

QUESTIONS

1. What does it mean for a Christian to be a *witness* in today's world?

2. What events caused Martin Avdyeeich to feel that life no longer had a meaning?

3. Where did he eventually find peace of mind?

4. Identify three ways in which Martin helped those whom he encountered.

5. What truth did Martin come to realise after reflecting on his experiences in the light of *Matthew* 25:40?

Case Study: Offering Friendship – The Samaritans

The Samaritans were founded in 1953 by Reverend Chad Varah, Rector of St Stephen's Anglican Church, Walbrook, in London. He had discovered that befriending by 'ordinary' people was often more acceptable than professional counselling for those who were considering committing *suicide* (i.e. taking their own lives). This befriending service is now available twenty-four hours a day, every day of the year, and has spread across the globe, with over 22,000 volunteers in some 200 branches.

▲ Chad Varah

All Samaritans obey the same strict rules:

■ *Absolute Confidentiality*

The Samaritans guarantee complete secrecy about the identity of callers and anything they discuss. Even if, for instance, a husband and wife or a parent and child contacted the Samaritans about the same matter separately, each can depend on total confidentiality.

Any request for information about people who avail of the service is refused. Answers to letters are in plain envelopes and do not mention the Samaritans. Personal callers are not acknowledged 'outside' by the volunteers if they encounter them, so as to preserve their privacy.

■ *Non-interference*

The caller is always 'in charge', and will never be contacted by the Samaritans or mentioned to any other agency or person unless he or she specifically requests it – and then only if the Samaritans' intervention is clearly needed by the caller.

■ *Acceptance of the caller's own beliefs and standards (no preaching)*

The Samaritans have no 'message' except that there is somebody ready to listen and befriend you, day or night, whenever you need it.

The Samaritans seek to offer sympathetic and concerned friendship to callers. Although their name comes from the well-known story of the Good Samaritan, not all of the volunteers are Christians.

The volunteers are ordinary people from all walks of life – from those in their twenties to senior citizens – who give up some of their free time to befriending others. Usually only their immediate family know that they are Samaritan volunteers, and they are known to callers and volunteers only by first names followed by a number, such as Michael twenty-four, Sarah six and so on.

Primarily, the Samaritans are there to help those who are suicidal or feel overwhelmed by feelings of loneliness and despair. *There is no problem that they will refuse to discuss.*

The Samaritans offer callers *time*, treat them with *respect* and take what they say *seriously*. They do *not* offer material help in cash or in kind, but will help people to contact those organisations that provide such help. They do *not* try to minimise people's problems nor do they offer vague assurances that things will work out easily. However, they do believe that talking things over in absolute confidence and privacy with someone who accepts you as you are can either help you to solve problems or else to discover new ways of living with an insoluble situation.

The Samaritans believe that by really listening to another human being in distress, they can help increase his/her sense of self-worth, help him/her to gain insight into the situation and reduce feelings of isolation and despair. They aim to help people see their problems in a new light and encourage them to find answers or to develop new attitudes that may help them to cope with their problems.

QUESTIONS

1. (a) Who founded the Samaritans? (b) Why did he do so?
2. (a) What do they offer? (b) What do they *not* offer?
3. What are the three strict rules that the Samaritans obey?
4. What is the importance of the service provided by the Samaritans?

Religious Communities

In the Catholic, Orthodox and Anglican churches, some people believe they are called to follow a different path in serving God in their community, rather than as a married or single person. They choose to enter *religious life*. This means that a man may enter a monastery and become a *monk* (either a *priest* or *brother*), and a woman may enter a convent and become a *nun* (also referred to as a *sister*).

Each monk or nun belongs to a specific religious order. These religious orders can be grouped under either of the following headings:

- ## Active Communities
  These religious orders have been founded with specific work in mind, such as teaching, nursing or missionary expansion.

- ## Contemplative Communities
  These religious orders devote their whole lives to prayer, study and physical work. They rarely leave the confines of their communities. Often they are only allowed to speak at particular times of the day. They may spend up to eight hours of each day at prayer.

The idea of religious communities has its origins in the early Christian Church in Jerusalem. Consider the following passage from the *New Testament*, where the early Christians expressed their *common unity* of faith.

> *The faithful all lived together and owned everything in common. They sold their goods and possessions and shared out the proceeds among themselves according to what each one needed.*
>
> *They went as a body to the Temple every day but met in their houses for the breaking of bread. They shared their food gladly and generously. They praised God and were looked up to by everyone.*
> Acts 2:44-7

We can see in this passage some of the elements of religious life today.

In all religious communities a monk or a nun lives under an arrangement known as the *rule* of that particular order. This rule offers detailed guidance as to how they can best live out their vocation (i.e. calling) as a monk or nun.

The best known and most influential monastic rule is *the Rule of St. Benedict*, set down in the sixth century.

Upon completion of their training, all monks and nuns must take the same three basic *vows* (i.e. solemn promises):

■ Poverty ■ Chastity ■ Obedience.

We shall examine each in turn.

Poverty

This means giving up all private possessions. It does not mean that a monk or a nun is left destitute. On the contrary, they are properly fed and clothed. This vow has more to do with freeing oneself from selfish attachments to possessions and living simply. It aims to encourage a monk or a nun to make the love and service of God the centre of his/her life.

Chastity

This involves making a choice not to get married and not to have sexual relations with anyone. A monk or a nun is asked to wholeheartedly commit him/herself to the worship of God and the service of a wider community.

Obedience

Here the monk or nun accepts the authority of his/her superior concerning the work he/she will do and where he/she will live. This vow of obedience enables a religious community to be *united* in its commitment to love God and neighbour.

QUESTIONS

1. What does it mean for a man or a woman *to enter religious life*?
2. Explain the difference between an *active* religious community and a *contemplative* religious community.
3. What is the best known and most influential monastic rule?
4. Explain the purpose of a monastic rule?
5. State the three basic vows all monks and nuns must take upon completing their training.

A Typical Day

Read the following extract in which Mother Teresa describes a typical day for the religious order she founded – the Missionaries of Charity.

Our lives are centred on the Eucharist and prayer. We begin our day with Mass and meditation.

After Mass and breakfast, some sisters go to the home for those who are dying, some go to the leper colonies, others go to the little schools we have in the slums, some take care of the preparation and distribution of food, some visit the homes of needy families and so on.

The sisters go all over the city. They travel everywhere with a rosary in hand. That is the way we pray in the streets. We do not go to the people without praying. The rosary has been our strength and our protection.

We always go in twos, and we come back around 12:30. At that time we have our lunch. After lunch, very often we have to do housework.

Then, for half an hour, every sister has to rest, because all the time they are on their feet. After that, we have an examination of conscience and pray.

At 2:00, we have spiritual reading for half an hour, and then a cup of tea.

At 3:00, the professed sisters [i.e. those who are fully trained and have taken their vows] again go out. Students remain in the house. They attend classes in theology.

Between 6:15 and 6:30, everybody comes back home.

From 6:30 to 7:30, we have adoration of the Blessed Sacrament. To be able to have this hour of adoration, we have not had to cut back on our work. We can work as many as ten or even twelve hours a day in service to the poor following this schedule.

At 7:30 we have dinner.

After dinner, for about twenty minutes, we have to prepare the work for next morning.

From 8:30 until 9:00, we have recreation. Everybody talks at the top of her lungs, after having worked all day long.

At 9:00, we go to the chapel for the night prayers and to prepare the meditations for the next morning.

Once a week ... we have a day of recollection. That day, the first-year novices [i.e. students] go out, because they are the ones who don't go out every day. Then all the professed sisters stay in for the day of recollection. That day we also go to confession and spend more time in adoration of the Blessed Sacrament. This is time when we can regain our strength and fill up our emptiness again with Jesus. That's why it is a very beautiful day.

Adapted from *A Life For God*, compiled by Lavonne Neff

QUESTIONS

1. Identify *four* forms of work in the community undertaken by the Missionaries of Charity.

2. Calculate how much time the sisters devote each day to each of the following:
   - Prayer
   - Study
   - Work
   - Recreation

3. Why do the sisters devote so much of their time to prayer?

Profile: Francis of Assisi, Servant of the Poor

Francis of Assisi (1181-1226) was born into a very rich merchant family. As a young man he spent money freely and generally had a good time.

Francis' life changed dramatically when he was twenty-one. After spending a few months as a prisoner-of-war in a nearby town he returned to Assisi ill and demoralised. It took him some while to get better, and during this time he became convinced that there must be more to life.

He tried to return to his old habits, but they did not seem so much fun any more. He'd been a Christian of a kind, but now he spent more and more time in prayer, thinking about the things of God. Slowly he became convinced that God was calling him to serve the poor.

After a pilgrimage to Rome he gave up his old ways completely, and spent his time caring for the lepers who lived outside the walls of Assisi, washing their sores and feeding them. He also rebuilt some broken-down old churches in the nearby countryside with his own hands. His father beat him, locked him up and then disowned him, completely astonished and horrified by what Francis was doing. But Francis did not care. He asked the Bishop of Assisi to protect him and gave everything he had back to his father (including the clothes he was wearing!). Francis carried on as before, living rough, caring for lepers and rebuilding churches.

One day Francis was listening to the Gospel at Mass in one of the churches he had rebuilt, when some words of Jesus struck home. In the reading, Jesus was telling the disciples to leave everything behind and preach the coming of God's Kingdom (Matthew 10:7-19).

At once Francis knew what he had to do. God was calling him to live with the poorest of the poor, to share their life completely and to preach the Gospel. And that is exactly what he did. He gave away what few remaining possessions he had and spent the rest of his life teaching, preaching and caring for those in poverty like his own.

At first many people thought he was mad, although some kind souls gave him enough scraps of food to keep him from starving. But soon his obvious holiness attracted others to join him: some as brothers (friars) sharing his life, some as nuns serving the poor in constant prayer, and some as married people living out a simple version of his 'rule' in the world. Today the Franciscans are the largest religious order in the Catholic Church.

Adapted from *Today's Issues and Christian Beliefs*

QUESTIONS

1. What events changed Francis of Assisi's whole outlook on life?
2. Why did Francis give away all his possessions?
3. Why were other people drawn to following Francis and live according to his rule?

CHAPTER SIX

SOURCES OF GUIDANCE

Introduction

The pace of change in today's world is astonishing. Although each new technological breakthrough brings many benefits, it can also raise new and challenging moral questions:

- *How should new discoveries in human genetics be put to use?*
- *Should animals be used to test the possible side effects of new drugs before they are prescribed for human use?*

It is not always easy for people to know what is the right thing to do. Furthermore, the wrong decision can have damaging consequences for oneself and others.

Love and Morality

In the Gospel stories Jesus revealed his deep concern for people. Christians today are called to follow his example to love God and their neighbour as themselves.

At this point, however, great care is needed. Unfortunately, human love can go wrong. For example, *eros* can deteriorate into a selfish desire for one's own pleasure, rather than a desire to share one's love with another person. Even when someone genuinely loves another person, there can still be problems:

- You could give bad advice because you were misinformed about some important issue. This could unintentionally cause harm to the person you love.
- In certain situations people can find it very difficult to know what is the right thing to do. The circumstances surrounding events such as a woman considering how to react to the news of a crisis pregnancy, or a family faced with the slow, painful death of a loved one, can raise powerful emotions that can affect one's judgment.
- People can deceive themselves. They can convince themselves that they are acting in a loving way, when in fact they are really being selfish, or even cowardly.

To truly love someone is to wish only good for that person and to resist anything that will harm him/her. This is an enormous responsibility.

People need *guidance* as to how they can best treat one another and live as harmoniously as possible in the complex world of the twenty-first century.

This is where *religion* has a vital role to play in people's lives.

QUESTIONS

1. Why is it important to know what is the right thing to do when faced with a moral decision?
2. Explain the meaning of the statement:

   Unfortunately, human love can go wrong.
3. What role can religion play in the complex world of the twenty-first century?

The Sources of Truth

Jesus commanded his apostles to

> *Go, make disciples of all the nations ... and teach them to observe all the commands I gave you.*
> *Matthew* 28:19-20

Catholics believe that the Gospel message has been faithfully handed on by means of two great sources of truth:

- *Sacred Scripture* and   - *Tradition*.

1 Sacred Scripture

The Catholic Church teaches that the *Bible* is the revealed word of God, written by people under the inspiration of the Holy Spirit.

> *God is the author of Sacred Scripture because he inspired its human authors; he acts in them and by means of them. He thus gives assurance that their writings teach without error his saving truth.*
> *Catechism of the Catholic Church* (136)

In the Ten Commandments and the Beatitudes, for example, God reveals how human beings should live.

2 Tradition

Catholics believe that while God speaks to people through sacred scripture, God also speaks through *tradition*. The word 'tradition' means

> *what is handed on from one generation to another.*

Tradition began with the small group of apostles gathered around Jesus.

> *What Christ entrusted to the apostles, they in turn handed on by their preaching and writing, under the inspiration of the Holy Spirit, to all generations ....*
> *Catechism of the Catholic Church* (96)

What has been handed on is not just a set of ideas but *a whole way of life*. Tradition includes:

- The *doctrines* (i.e. teachings) of the Church expressed in the Apostles' Creed and the Nicene Creed.

- The insights of the Church's saints and scholars, particularly *Augustine of Hippo* and Thomas Aquinas.

- The worship of God in the seven sacraments, which has led many people into a deeper loving relationship with God and each other.

- The heroic example of holy men and holy women who inspire others to follow the way of Jesus.

- The living and active faith of all members of the Catholic Church over the centuries, and the institutions they established to carry out the Church's mission to spread the Gospel.

Tradition is the Catholic Church living out its understanding of and faith in Jesus Christ.

Augustine of Hippo
➡

Reflection

Scripture and tradition are *not* separate elements in the life of the Catholic Church.

It teaches that scripture and tradition form an essential *unity*. Both are sources of the *one* divine revelation of God to human beings.

Consider the following:

- Scripture is the inspired Word of God.
- Tradition is the process by which the Church hands on the faith of Catholics.

In the Catholic Church, scripture and tradition are given *equal* honour.

QUESTIONS

1. Use the words listed below to fill in the missing words in the spaces provided.

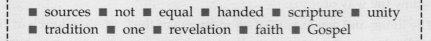

- sources ■ not ■ equal ■ handed ■ scripture ■ unity
- tradition ■ one ■ revelation ■ faith ■ Gospel

Catholics believe that the _____ message has been faithfully

QUESTIONS CONTD

_____ on by means of two great _____ of truth:

- Sacred scripture and ■ Tradition.

Scripture and tradition are _____ separate elements in the life of the Church. They form an essential _____. Both are sources of the _____ divine _____ of God to human beings.

- _____ is the inspired Word of God.

- _____ is the process by which the Church hands on the _____ of Catholics.

In the Catholic Church, scripture and tradition are given _____ honour.

2. Identify which of the following statements are *true* and which are *false*.

   (a) The *Bible* is the revealed word of God written by people under the inspiration of the Pope.

   (b) The word *tradition* means *what is handed on from one generation to another*.

   (c) Tradition began with a small group of apostles gathered around Peter.

   (d) Tradition not only hands on a set of ideas but a whole way of life.

   (e) Augustine of Hippo and Thomas Aquinas are important Christian saints and scholars.

The Magisterium

The task of *interpreting* sacred scripture and tradition to guide the belief and behaviour of Catholics is the responsibility of the *Magisterium*. The word 'magisterium' comes from the Latin word *magister* meaning *teacher*.

In a broad sense, this teaching role belongs to all members of the Catholic Church, as all are called to communicate the message of Jesus by what they say and do.

Strictly speaking, however, the term *magisterium* is used to refer to the Pope and the college of bishops under his leadership, who exercise their official role as teachers of the Catholic faith.

The world's Catholic bishops gather in
Rome under the leadership of the Pope.
▼

*The task of interpreting the word of God authentically has been
entrusted solely to the Magisterium of the Church, that is, to the
Pope and to the bishops in communion with him.*
Catechism of the Catholic Church (100)

Catholics make an important distinction between:

■ the *Extraordinary* Magisterium

  and

■ the *Ordinary* Magisterium.

1 The Extraordinary Magisterium

This occurs on rare occasions when the Pope makes a solemn declaration *ex
cathedra*, i.e. using his full authority as successor of the apostle Peter, on a
matter vital to the faith or morals of the Church.

    The Pope can do so either alone or in an Ecumenical (i.e. general) Council
where the world's Catholic bishops are united under his leadership.

    Catholics believe that the decision reached is protected from any error by
the power of the Holy Spirit. As a result, the Pope is said to be *infallible* (from
the Latin meaning *unable to deceive*) on matters of faith and morals.

    Any teachings declared infallible are called *dogmas* of the Church and they
must be unreservedly accepted by all Catholics.

2 The Ordinary Magisterium

This consists of the guidance on matters of Church teaching offered by the Pope and the bishops by means of public statements and written documents. The most important of these documents is a special letter written by the Pope called a *papal encyclical*.

These statements should be treated with respect and carefully studied by Catholics. They provide a clear, unified Catholic response to important moral issues such as abortion, capital punishment, crime, divorce and so on.

Although these statements and documents produced by the Ordinary Magisterium are *not* considered infallible, Catholics are expected to acknowledge the Ordinary Magisterium as their guide regarding what to believe and how to behave.

Catholics believe that God continues to speak through the teachings of the Catholic Church. As a result, Catholics should respect and accept the teachings of the Ordinary Magisterium.

When a Catholic wants to know whether something is the right or the wrong thing to do, he/she is expected to carefully consider and follow the teaching of the Catholic Church on this matter.

▲
Statue of the first pope, the Apostle Peter, in St Peter's Basilica, Rome

Importance of Magisterium

The Magisterium plays a key role in the life of the Catholic Church. As Thomas Zanzig has written:

> *The teaching authority of the Pope with the bishops is one important way that the Church has been able to keep unity in the midst of the diverse conditions, customs and ways of thinking among Catholic people around the world.*

QUESTIONS

1. Write a brief note on the *Magisterium* of the Catholic Church.
   In your answer:
   - Explain the origin of the word *Magisterium*.
   - Identify those to whom it refers.
   - Outline the task of the *Magisterium*.

2. Use the words listed below to fill in the missing words in the spaces provided.

   > - Pope ■ successor ■ morals ■ rare ■ Peter
   > - Ecumenical ■ authority ■ vital ■ bishops

   The Extraordinary Magisterium occurs on _____ occasions when the

   _____ makes a solemn declaration *ex cathedra*, i.e. using his full

   _____ as _____ of the apostle _____, on a matter _____ to

   the faith and _____ of the Church. The Pope can do so either alone

   or in an _____ council, where the Catholic _____ are

   united under his leadership.

3. Explain the meaning of the word *infallible*.

4. Why do Catholics believe that the Pope is infallible when speaking *ex cathedra* on matters of faith and morals?

5. What is a *dogma*?

6. What is a *papal encyclical*?

7. Use the words listed below to fill in the missing words in the spaces provided.

   > - teachings ■ acknowledge ■ Magisterium ■ unified
   > - behave ■ moral ■ not ■ accept ■ guide ■ studied

   The statements of the Ordinary _____ should be treated with

   respect and carefully ____. They provide a clear, _____ Catholic

QUESTIONS CONTD

response to important _____ issues. Although these statements

are _____ considered infallible, Catholics are expected to _____ the

Ordinary Magisterium as their _____ regarding what to believe

and how to _____. Catholics believe that God continues to speak

through the _____ of the Catholic Church. As a result, Catholics

should respect and _____ the teaching of the Ordinary Magisterium.

CHAPTER SEVEN

CONSCIENCE

Introduction

It is Saturday morning at a busy shopping centre. A shopper accidentally drops his wallet on the ground without realising it. He leaves it behind him. It contains two hundred euros in cash. If someone finds it, what should they do?

Consider how these three people respond to this situation:

- **Alan** puts the wallet in his pocket. He says, '*OK, so it's not mine, but the owner should have been more careful. Finders, keepers!*'

- **Susan** thinks that no one has noticed her picking up the wallet. So she decides to keep the money. She says, '*Hard luck for the owner, but I could really use this money.*'

- **Michael** finds the money. He says, '*I could really use the money, but it's not mine to keep.*' Michael takes it to the centre's management office and leaves it for the owner to claim.

Both Alan and Susan know that what they have chosen to do is *wrong*. Michael could have easily pocketed the money just as they did. However, unlike them, Michael values *honesty*. He realises that to keep the money would be stealing. He hands it in for the owner to reclaim. Michael chooses to do good rather than evil.

People often remark that someone like Michael *has a conscience*.

The Meaning of Conscience

What precisely is conscience?

The Catholic Church teaches that conscience is *the voice of God speaking in the individual*. The great theologian Thomas Aquinas explained what this means.

Conscience is not...

■ Some kind of special revelation from God before a person makes a moral decision.

Conscience is not...

■ Some kind of mysterious, independent thing inside each person.

Conscience is...

■ *A person's ability to apply his/her values to a particular moral problem and make a decision about what is the right thing to do.*

Conscience is *a gift* given by God to human beings. When a person uses this gift correctly to make good moral decisions, then God *speaks* to him/her.

The Formation of Conscience

People's families, and all those who influence their values as they are growing up, have an important role to play in the development of their individual consciences.

This is why the Catholic Church places great emphasis on the responsibility of parents to develop the consciences of children by the example they set, and on individuals to develop their own conscience through *prayer*, *study* and *good actions*.

> *A well-formed conscience is upright and truthful. It formulates its judgments according to reason, in conformity with the true good willed by the wisdom of the Creator. Everyone must avail himself of the means to form his conscience.*
> *Catechism of the Catholic Church (1798)*

Conscience in Action

Normally, our conscience operates with such remarkable speed and efficiency that we are rarely aware of how it functions. Let us take a slow-motion example to illustrate how we can apply a general moral principle to a particular moral problem:

■ *Problem:* I enter a shop. The counter is unattended. I am tempted to take a bar of chocolate without paying for it.

■ *Principle:* But it is wrong to steal.

■ *Conclusion:* Therefore, if I take this bar of chocolate without paying for it, I am doing something wrong.

■ *Decision*: A good person would then say, 'I wish to help people. I do not want to cause harm to another person, so I will not steal this item. If I want it and if I can afford it, I will purchase it.'

QUESTIONS

1. What is meant by *conscience*?
2. Explain the meaning of the following statement:
    Conscience is the voice of God speaking in each individual.
3. What are the *three ways* in which a person may develop his/her own conscience?

JOURNAL WORK

Read the following statement:
    Some people believe that our society is becoming so obsessed with wealth and pleasure that conscience is being stifled and that a person like Michael, in the opening story, is the exception today.
Do you agree/disagree? Explain your answer.

Why Be Honest?

An honest person is one who tries to do what is right, even when it works to his/her own disadvantage. Honesty involves being truthful with oneself and recognising one's obligation to God and to other people. Honesty has no time for lying, cheating or the desire to succeed at any price.

Even so, dishonesty is more widespread in our world than anyone would want it to be. We are not talking here about a 'little white lie' told to spare the feelings of a friend whose taste in hairstyles or clothing does not match up to one's own particular fashion sense. We are dealing here with more serious and important issues.

Frequently, people ask the question, '*Why be honest*?' Christians offer these answers:

- Because God demands it of us (the Eighth Commandment).
- Because it is the basis for all genuine human relationships. Without honesty relationships disintegrate because there is a lack of trust.
- Because dishonesty creates situations that tempt a person to invent more lies to cover up the ones they have already told, so making a bad situation even worse.
- Because dishonest acts, such as shoplifting, bribery and fraudulent insurance claims, lead to higher costs which affect everyone.

A morally *mature* person is one who ·

- thinks before acting;
- honestly evaluates a situation;
- considers the consequences of his/her actions for both him/herself and others;
- decides on a course of action that is in accordance with his/her values.

Difficulties

People need to be aware, however, that certain things can cloud their judgment and make it difficult for them to know what is the right choice to make.

There are four main causes of error:

1. Where people are *ignorant* (unaware) of the true nature of the problem facing them, either because they did not or could not get all the advice or information they needed.

2. Where people allow their *emotions* to unduly influence their decision-making. Just because something makes you *feel* good or bad about doing something does *not* guarantee that it is the right thing to do.

3. When people do something for the sake of *conformity*, in order to win favour with others. Just because everyone else is either for or against something does not make it right.

4. Where people make *a mistake in their reasoning*, e.g.

   Problem: War involves killing people.
   Principle: It is always wrong to kill another person.
   Conclusion: Therefore, war is wrong.

The problem here is that this principle is *not* true for *every* situation. In some circumstances it may, regrettably, be both necessary and correct to take a human life, for example in defence of oneself or one's loved ones in times of extreme danger, when there is *no other* course of action open to you.

QUESTIONS

1. (a) Give one example of *conformist behaviour* (i.e. going along with the crowd).
   (b) Why do people think and behave in this way?
2. In what circumstances might it *regrettably* be both necessary and correct to take a human life?

Making a Moral Decision

What follows is a checklist of questions people should ask themselves before making an *important* moral decision.

- Begin by defining the problem. What exactly is the issue at stake?
- Check that you have all the relevant facts.
- Look for advice. Find out what your religion teaches and pray for guidance.

- Consider what the law of the state says.

- Consider your motives for making a particular choice. Are you only suiting yourself? Are you taking others into account?

- What are the methods open to you? Remember, the thing you want to achieve (the end) never justifies the use of *any* method you want to use (the means). There are certain actions (e.g. *murder* or *rape*) which are morally wrong and can *never* be justified.

▲
Don't just blindly follow the pack. Think before acting.

- What are the likely *effects* of a particular course of action on both yourself and other people?

Only *after* going through this process of careful reflection about what is the right thing to do, should a person act according to his/her conscience.

Most people only do this when faced with a *major* decision. As mentioned earlier, when faced with most minor decisions people do not consciously use this process.

QUESTION

1. When should a person act according to his/her conscience?

JOURNAL WORK

Imagine you are a member of a group campaigning against the emissions from a nuclear power plant.

There is some evidence that it is causing damage to the health of the local people and slowly destroying their environment.

Your group leader declares that swift, violent action is necessary to stop this. He claims that a small explosive device, placed inside the main control room, would disable the entire plant and end the emissions.

Some members of the group think that this kind of action is the only solution. But you doubt if this really is the best course of action. Before

JOURNAL WORK CONTD.

deciding to accept or reject the idea of going ahead with the plan, consider the following:

A. Examine the *consequences* of the group leader's plan for:
- Your group – this action is against the law.
- The employees – what about their jobs?
- The local community – could the explosion cause harmful material to escape into the air and cause widespread illness or death?
- The local environment – will it make matters better or worse?

B. Can you suggest a *better* way to end this pollution *without* using violence?

The Price of Conscience

The Catholic Church teaches that each person

> *has the right to act in conscience and in freedom so as personally to make moral decisions.*
> Catechism of the Catholic Church (1782)

People should always try to:
- act in accordance with their values;
- remain faithful to the teachings of their religion;
- do everything possible to fully inform their consciences;
  and
- follow their consciences when confronted with a moral decision.

No one should be forced to act against his/her properly informed conscience.

However, to follow one's conscience may cost a person dearly. Consider the story of Thomas More.

Profile: Thomas More

Robert Bolt wrote a famous play called *A Man for All Seasons*, which has also been made into an Oscar-winning film. It tells the story of Sir Thomas More who, in the sixteenth century, was, for a time, Chancellor (i.e. Prime Minister) of England and a close friend of King Henry VIII.

Thomas was a widely renowned scholar and lawyer. He was the internationally respected author of several books, most notably his classic work *Utopia*. Thomas was also a deeply religious person.

As long as England remained Catholic and Henry VIII was a Catholic king, Thomas More was treated with respect and was bestowed with many honours. Then, Henry VIII decided to divorce his first wife, Catherine of Aragon, and to break away from the Catholic Church. The king, and not the Pope, would in future be head of the Church in England.

▲
King Henry VIII   Thomas More ➡

Henry VIII wanted the support of his Chancellor, Thomas More. But Thomas could not in conscience agree with the king's decision. He wanted to remain faithful to God and true to himself. He refused to support Henry VIII's policy, but he felt it wise not to publicly declare his opposition.

On 17 May 1532, Thomas More resigned from his post as Chancellor and silently withdrew from public life. He kept his opinions and his thoughts to himself.

For a time it seemed as though his silence would save his life. But Thomas's refusal to take part in Henry VIII's government was taken by many people as a powerful statement of his disapproval of the king's action. One of the characters in Bolt's play, when he speaks of Thomas's silence, explains the power that Thomas More had over the Europe of the day, *That man's silence is bellowing all over Europe.*

The decision was made by the king's ministers to force Thomas More to declare himself for or against the king's actions. In April 1534, Thomas was arrested on a charge of treason and imprisoned in the Tower of London. He still refused to take the oath of allegiance recognising the king, and not the Pope, as the head of the English Church.

Thomas More was put on trial for his life. If found guilty of treason he would be executed. The trial was a farce. Its sole purpose was to discredit Thomas and make him appear to be disloyal, dishonest and treacherous.

Thomas remained true to his conscience. He refused to swear an oath to the succession of the King and Queen Anne Boleyn's child. The court declared Thomas guilty of treason after accepting the false evidence of several witnesses. He was beheaded on 6 July 1543. Before his death he told those assembled to witness his execution that, *I die the king's good servant, but God's first.*

Thomas More was declared a saint and martyr (i.e. someone who died for his beliefs) by the Catholic Church in 1936. Pope John Paul II declared him the patron saint of politicians in 2001.

QUESTIONS

1. What high office did Sir Thomas More hold in King Henry VIII's government?
2. Which decision by King Henry VIII led Thomas More to resign his office?
3. Why did King Henry VIII want Thomas More to publicly support his actions?
4. Why did Thomas More refuse to do this?
5. Explain what Thomas More meant when he said, 'I die the king's good servant, but God's first'.

CHAPTER EIGHT

ORIGINAL SIN

Introduction

A person may know where to find good advice, and even know what is the right thing to do. But in the end, it all comes down to having the courage of one's convictions, i.e to actually *apply* one's values when one is confronted with a situation that offers a choice.

However, as we saw in the case of Thomas More, this can extract a high price and it seems that few people are willing to pay it.

Having the Courage of One's Convictions

▲ Nikita Khrushchev

Joseph Stalin ruled over the people of Russia with an iron fist from 1927 until his death in 1953. Some historians believe that he was responsible for the deaths of over sixteen million of his own people.

Three years after his death, Stalin's successor as Russia's leader, Nikita Khrushchev, made a speech to the annual congress of the ruling Communist Party. Khrushchev amazed all those present by condemning Stalin's reign of terror over Russia. No one had dared to speak in this way for many years.

When he finished his speech, Khrushchev began to step down from the speaker's rostrum. The entire audience sat there in a stunned silence. Just then, a man shouted up from the middle of the packed auditorium, '*So, why didn't you do something at the time to stop Stalin?*' Khrushchev had been a minister in Stalin's government.

This question both angered and embarrassed Khrushchev. He looked up, scanned the audience and shouted back, '*Who said that?*' There was total silence. No one replied. After a minute or so, Khrushchev spoke into the microphone again, '*There now, you have your answer!*'

It is all very well to ask someone else why he/she did not do the brave thing. Each person should look to his/her own moral courage first, before being willing to criticise others.

Human Weakness

People often find it difficult to do the right thing. Paul wrote about his own experience of this:

> *I cannot understand my own behaviour. I fail to carry out the things I want to do, and I find myself doing the very thing I hate.*
> Romans 7:15-16

When confronted with a difficult moral choice, every human being experiences this pull in opposite directions: to stand one's ground and do what is right, or to turn away and do what is wrong. It is difficult to choose and follow the path of good; it is much easier to take the path of least resistance and give in to some passing desire. It takes courage to think differently to others, to choose to live by different values, to believe what others may dismiss and to do the right thing.

QUESTIONS

Read the following passage by Dr Martin Luther King Jnr.

> *Courage is an inner resolution to go forward despite obstacles; cowardice is submissive surrender to circumstances.*
>
> *Courage breeds creativity; cowardice produces destruction. Courage faces fear and masters it; cowardice represses fear and is mastered by it ....*
>
> *Cowardice asks the question, is it safe? Expediency asks the question, is it politic? Vanity asks the question, is it popular?*
>
> *But conscience asks the question, is it right? And there comes a time when one must take a position that is neither safe, nor politic, nor popular, but one must take it because it is right.*

QUESTIONS CONTD.

1. What does Dr King mean by *cowardice*?
2. What does he mean by *courage*?
3. What is the question asked by conscience?

Original Sin

Christians acknowledge that *all* people find choosing and doing good instead of evil to be a real challenge.

Christians do *not* believe, however, that God created human beings with some kind of built-in tendency to do bad things. Rather, they believe that God can only create what is *good*. Therefore, all people are created good. Yet experience shows that people often find it difficult to do good and avoid evil. Why?

The key to answering this question can be found in the story of *the Fall* as recounted in the *Old Testament* book of *Genesis*, chapter three.

This tells of how Adam and Eve gave in to temptation, deliberately disobeyed God and as a result were banished forever from the Garden of Eden.

We should *not* consider this story to be a literal historical account. Whatever its actual historical details, however, this is a very important story which contains a profound message.

The study of *Genesis* 3:1-21 will help us to understand the doctrine (i.e. teaching) of *Original Sin*.

- The story of Adam and Eve is called *the Fall*. It tells how the first humans chose to disobey God and do what they knew to be wrong. As a result they brought *sin* (i.e. wrongdoing) into the world.

- Our earliest ancestors acted out of pride and selfishness, and *fell away* from the state of innocent goodness in which God had wanted them to live.

- This first sin, by the first human beings, is called the *original* sin. It affected all of human society. The effects of this original sin were passed on from one generation to the next down through history. It is because of this that human beings are *weak* in their resolve to do good and avoid evil.

Our earliest ancestors turned away from God and threw away the gift of perfect happiness, which Christians believe can only be found by living the way God wants us to live.

QUESTIONS

1. Why is this story in *Genesis* 3:1–21 known as *the Fall*?
2. Why is the sin first committed by our earliest ancestors known as *original sin*?
3. What has been the effect of this *original sin* on all human beings since then?

JOURNAL WORK

Consider each of the following points in the story of *the Fall*:

(a) *Temptation is subtle, appealing to pride.*
   Give examples from your own experience of temptations which appeal to pride.

(b) *Having done wrong, Eve wants someone to share her wrongdoing and tempts the person closest to her.*
   Check in any newspaper how many of the cases brought before a court involve more than one person accused of committing a crime.

(c) *When they realise they are not as clever as they thought, Adam and Eve try to hide themselves.*
   How do people try to hide wrongdoing in ordinary daily life?

(d) *They cannot face God and blame everyone but themselves.*
   Can you identify any situations reported in the news media where people say, 'It wasn't me'! and are unwilling to face up to their guilt?

(e) *God does not leave them alone in their sin. He visits them.*
   How does God 'visit', i.e. make himself known to, people today?

Reason for Hope

God did not create human beings and then leave us to flounder about without hope.
   Christians believe that:

Adam and Eve cast out of the Garden of Eden, *The Expulsion from Paradise* by Masaccio ➡

- God rescued our world from sin by becoming a human being in Jesus Christ.
- Jesus has shown people the way that God always intended them to live, and the way in which they can achieve peace with God and with one other.
- Jesus invites people to follow him, but does not force anyone. The choice is up to each individual to make.
- People are called to pursue lives of *virtue*, i.e. to develop and act upon their God-given capacity for treating each other with compassion, honesty, love and respect.

Jesus by El Greco

- However, people cannot achieve this entirely by their own efforts. They need God's *grace* (i.e. loving help) to guide and strengthen them to do good and avoid doing evil.

If people choose to follow Jesus, help is at hand, as Rowanne Pascoe and John Redford have written:

> *Baptism into the Christian community signifies our acceptance of, and frees us from, Original Sin; but we are still weak. We need the daily strength of the Holy Spirit to conquer that weakness, and the support of each other. That is one important reason why we need to belong to the Church, the community of believers.*
>
> *Faith Alive*

QUESTIONS

1. What do Christians believe about the role of Jesus in their struggle to live good and worthwhile lives?
2. (a) What is meant by *God's grace*? (b) Why do people need it?

CHAPTER NINE

SIN AND FORGIVENESS

Introduction

Human beings are by nature social creatures. Our lives consist largely of a complex web of relationships with other people. In these relationships, people experience a moral obligation to behave in certain ways towards one another. However, it requires *courage* to do the right thing when confronted with a moral choice.

   Whenever people *selfishly* disregard their obligations to others, they enter the realm of *actual sin*.

Actual Sin

We may define *actual sin* as

any freely chosen, deliberately intended and selfish action whose consequences one desires, which inflicts harm on one's neighbours and oneself.

In damaging one's relationship with another person, one damages one's relationship with *God*. The degree of damage depends on the *seriousness* of the sin committed.

> **N.B.**
> Actual sin is *different* from original sin, yet *related* to it. It is because human beings have to struggle within themselves to do good and avoid evil that they are prone to commit actual sin.

QUESTIONS

1. What is *actual sin*?

2. How does actual sin damage one's relationship with *God*?

3. Read the following story.

When Leonardo da Vinci was painting his masterpiece, *The Last Supper*, he looked for a model for his Christ. At last, he located a chorister in one of the churches of Rome who was handsome in life and features, a young man named Pietro Bandinelli. Years passed, and the painting was unfinished. All the disciples had been painted except one – Judas Iscariot. Now da Vinci started to look for a man whose face was hardened and distorted by sin – and at last he found a beggar on the streets of Milan with a face so villainous that da Vinci shuddered when he looked at him. He hired the man to sit for him as he painted the face of Judas on his canvas. When he was about to dismiss the man, da Vinci said, 'I have not yet found out your name.' The man answered, 'I am Pietro Bandinelli. I also sat for you as your model of Christ.'

During his forty days in the desert Jesus resisted the temptations of Satan. How do we deal with the temptation to sin? If we allow sin to take over our lives, it will destroy the image of Christ in us, just as it destroyed the image of Christ in the young Pietro Bandinelli.

The Sunday Message

Answer the following questions:

(a) Describe Pietro Bandinelli's appearance as a young man.

(b) Why did Leonardo da Vinci not recognise him when he met him many years later?

(c) What does this story tell you about the impact of sin on a person's life?

The Last Supper by Da Vinci ➡

Kinds of Sins

◄ *The Temptation of St Anthony* by Terniers

Catholics believe that there are *two* kinds of actual sin:

   (i) *Venial sin*, and (ii) *Mortal sin*.

Venial sin is *any action a person commits that weakens his/her relationship with God*. It is a refusal to live as God intends us to live and usually stems from *pride* and *selfishness*, from a refusal to love. Venial sin can lead to a gradual movement away from God. Therefore, it can be responsible for the eventual breakdown of a person's relationship with God.

   Mortal sin, on the other hand, is *any seriously wrongful act by which a person destroys his/her relationship with God*. To be guilty of mortal sin, a person must freely, deliberately and with full knowledge of its consequences, commit a very serious offence against both God and other people. It is a deliberate turning away from the love of God.

QUESTIONS

1. Explain the difference between mortal and venial sin.

2. Read the following story, then answer the questions below.

   Two men once visited a holy man to ask his advice. 'We have done wrong actions,' they said, 'and our consciences are troubled. Can you tell us what we must do so that we may be forgiven and feel clear of our guilt?'

   'Tell me of your wrongdoings,' said the old man. The first man said, 'I have committed a great and grievous sin.'

   'What about you?' the holy man asked the second. 'Oh,' he said, 'I have done quite a number of wrong things, but they are all quite small, and not at all important.' The holy man considered for a while. 'This is what you must do,' he said at last. 'Each of you must go and bring me a stone for each of his misdeeds.'

   Off went the men, and presently the first came back staggering with an enormous boulder, so heavy that he could hardly lift it, and with a groan he let it fall in front of the holy man. Then along came the second, cheerfully carrying a bag of small pebbles. This he also laid at the feet of the saint.

   'Now,' said the holy man, 'take all those stones and put them back where you found them.'

   The first man shouldered his rock again, and staggered back to the place from which he had brought it. But the second man could only remember where a few of his pebbles had lain. After some time, he came back, and said that the task was too difficult.

   'You must know,' said the old man, 'that sins are like these stones. If a man has committed a great sin, it lies like a heavy stone on his conscience; but if he is truly sorry, he is forgiven and the load is taken away. But if a man is constantly doing small things that are wrong, he does not feel any very great load of guilt, and so he is not sorry, and remains a sinner. So, you see, my son, it is as important to avoid little sins as big ones.'

   (a) What do you think is the message of this story?

   (b) What point does it make about the impact of our sins on the lives of both other people and ourselves?

The Ways of Committing Sin

A person can commit a sin in either of *two* ways:

(i)   By *commission* – when one deliberately does something one knows one should not.

(ii) By *omission* – when one deliberately *neglects* to do something one knows one should do.

Sin by Commission

In 1854, the passenger ship Artic was crossing the North Atlantic when it struck an iceberg. The ship began to sink. There were not enough lifeboats for everyone on board, so the captain gave the order, 'Women and children first!'

However, most of the crew disobeyed his command. Some of them broke into the ship's armoury and seized weapons. These crew members then held the women and children at gunpoint while they took control of the lifeboats.

Most of the crew survived the sinking, but none of the women or children survived.

T. Deary, *True Disaster Stories*

Sin by Omission

The funeral of Francis McNamara, seven, who lost a two-day fight for life after a crayon lodged in his windpipe, will be held on Monday.

The boy died last Thursday night at a hospital. He swallowed the crayon on his way home in a school bus. Motorists drove by while the bus driver frantically waved for help.

Finally, in desperation, the bus driver jumped in front of a motorist who was forced to stop. But the man refused to take the youngster to a hospital, saying he would be 'late for work'.

The bus driver, seeking a quicker trip than the bus could make, waved down another driver, who took Francis to Fairlawn Hospital in nearby Worcester. There a doctor quickly opened the boy's chest and massaged his heart to keep him alive.

Dr. Chang Kim then ordered surgery, but it was too late. Doctors said the boy died from brain damage suffered during the minutes his heart had stopped beating.

Adapted from M. Link, *Man in the Modern World*

N.B.
It is important to remember that Christians believe that all people are sinners to a greater or lesser extent. No one has the right to feel superior. One may condemn the *act* but *not* the *person*. No one has the right to condemn another.

Choosing to Face the Moral Challenge

In contrast to the two cases examined above, consider the story of *Oskar Schindler*, who risked his life on numerous occasions as he sought to save the lives of over a thousand Jewish men, women and children who worked in his factory. He prevented them from being murdered by Hitler's SS. Schindler used every possible trick and resource he could think of to save those people.

▲
Liam Neeson as Oskar Schindler in the film *Schindler's List*

This took enormous courage at a time in which most people around him either actively or tacitly supported the mass murder of the concentration camps. Had Schlinder's activities been discovered, he would surely have been executed. Yet he was willing to take the risk. He believed it was a risk *worth taking*.

QUESTIONS

1. Using the two stories set out above explain the difference between
   (a) *sin by commission* and (b) *sin by omission*.
2. (a) Why do you think Oskar Schindler did what he did?
   (b) Why didn't more people do the same?

Forgiveness

During his earthly ministry, Jesus called on people to

> *Repent and believe the Good News!*

He said that God had unlimited love for even the worst of us and forgave the sins of all those who genuinely wanted to reform their lives.

In the *Our Father*, Jesus taught his followers to pray:

> *Forgive us our trespasses (i.e. sins), as we forgive those who trespass against us.*

We will now examine the two aspects of this prayer.

▼ *The Return of the Prodigal Son* by Rembrandt

Forgive us our trespasses

The story of the *Prodigal Son* (*Luke* 15:11-32) is familiar to most people. But this familiarity can often blind people to its true significance.

Jesus wished all to know that, like the wayward son of the story, if people are genuinely sorry and want to reform their lives, God will forgive their sin. Though they may turn their backs on God and walk away, God remains loving and forgiving, offering them the chance to repair the damage they have done to their relationship with God and with those around them. It is never too late to repent as far as God is concerned.

Some people, however, cannot understand a feeling of guilt. They have so dulled their conscience that they apparently have no guilt feelings at all. When they are brought to court for a violent crime, they will insist either (a) *they did not do it*, or (b) *the victim forced them to do it*. Sometimes they will even try to convince themselves that their victims *wanted* them to harm them. This pattern of behaviour is quite common with violent criminals. Unlike the Prodigal Son, they cannot admit either to themselves or to others their responsibility for their evil actions. The admission of personal responsibility for having harmed another person is the first, vital step towards finding forgiveness.

As we forgive those who trespass against us

Jesus said that if people want God to forgive them, then they too must be prepared to forgive those who have offended them.

Consider the parable of the *Unforgiving Servant* (*Matthew* 18:22-25).

The parable has three main characters: a king and two servants. One servant owes the king a huge amount of money, in today's terms, several million pounds. He tearfully promises to repay it, and pleads for time. The king feels so sorry for him that he cancels the entire debt. But the servant learns nothing from his experience. On his way home, he meets another servant, one who owes him money, a paltry sum of about twenty pounds. His colleague pleads with him for time to repay it. But he will have none of it; instead, he has him thrown into prison.

When the king hears what has happened, he summons the unforgiving servant and tells him angrily, 'I cancelled your huge debt out of compassion. Should you not have done the same?' Then, the king has him thrown into prison until he can repay the debt in full.

In the parable, God is the king, and we are the servants. Like the first servant, we beg for mercy, and He gives a total pardon. God is the great forgiver. But, like the first servant, we can take God's forgiveness for granted. We can forget how merciful God is to us and fail to show that mercy to others, just as the first servant failed to show compassion towards his colleague. But the message of the parable is clear. Just as God is generous with us, so too must we be generous with one another. Indeed, we must forgive each other if we expect God to forgive us.

The Sunday Message

Forgiving those who have offended us or harmed us can often be far from easy. It can demand great courage and strength.

On November 6, 1987, at the cenotaph in Enniskillen, an IRA bomb killed eleven people, including three couples, and injured sixty.

Gordon Wilson and his daughter Marie, a nurse, were buried in the rubble. She stretched out her hand to him. 'Is that you Daddy?' 'Yes, dear. Are you all right?' He repeated the question four more times before she said – her last words – 'Daddy, I love you very much.'

Cars damaged in bomb blast ▼

Interviewed the next day, he said, 'I bear no ill will .... She was a great girl. She's in heaven now. We will meet again.'

What Alf McCreary, Mr Wilson's biographer, later revealed is that originally he did not forgive his daughter's murderers. He only said he had no ill will towards them. Forgiving them took time and effort and constant prayer.

Irish Independent

Forgiveness does *not* mean letting people walk all over us. Each person is entitled to justice and for those who have caused harm to be held accountable for their actions.

However, Jesus taught that to refuse to forgive and to seek revenge, will only destroy a person from within. Forgiveness is vital.

Jesus makes clear that if people want to receive God's forgiveness, they must show:

■ a genuine sorrow for what they have done;

■ a readiness to forgive those who have offended them;

■ a willingness to change their way of life and to make amends.

QUESTIONS

1. What does the parable of the *Prodigal Son* say about God's forgiveness?

2. Summarise the parable of the *Unforgiving Servant* and explain what it says about forgiving others.

3. Read the story of Gordon Wilson once more. If more people followed his example and refused to seek revenge, how could that help to resolve conflicts between people and nations?

4. What are *three* things that Jesus said are required to receive God's forgiveness?

Profile: St Patrick, A Model of Forgiveness

Read the following article by Fionnuala Ní Chuill.

Even a quick glance through *St Patrick's Confession* leaves us with a host of images for reflection. These images are conjured up by such words as captured, kidnapped, hostage, slave, God, betrayal and public humiliation. The vocabulary is as familiar to us today as it was to our ancestors in the fifth century. Basically, human nature remains very much the same.

Hence, it is no surprise to learn that Patrick suffered at the hands of others and that he had his enemies. Patrick could not change the many situations in which he found himself, so, how did he cope?

Patrick was a man of deep personal prayer. Prayer, to be genuine, must be lived out in practice. Did Patrick, in his personal life, give witness to the divine command to 'Love your enemies'? Did he manage to really forgive his enemies? *St Patrick's Confession* answers all these questions and in so doing, gives us an insight into the sincerity of his relationship with God. For Patrick loved much and forgave much.

Patrick grew up happily in Roman Britain. He was a freeborn citizen of the Roman Empire and a Christian. At the age of sixteen disaster struck. Patrick was kidnapped, brought to Ireland and sold as a slave. It was a traumatic change for the teenager: he was suddenly cut off from his family, friends and homeland; his education was disrupted; and he lost his rights as a free man. His sense of outrage and righteous anger, in the face of the injustice meted out to him, must have been immense.

Unable to communicate in the foreign language of the Irish, Patrick, in his anger and utter helplessness, cried out to God. Gradually, as he opened up his heart in prayer, he discovered a God who cared about him and to whom he could relate:

> 'God showed concern for my weakness, and pity for my youth and ignorance; he watched over me before I got to know him and before I was able to distinguish good from evil. In fact he protected me and comforted me as a father would his son.'

These were the early years of Patrick's captivity and the period that led to his conversion,

> 'The Lord made me aware of my unbelief that I might at last advert to my sins and turn wholeheartedly to the Lord my God.'

What Patrick could not change, he had to accept. In his surrender, he turned *wholeheartedly* to God and learned to forgive and love his enemies. Patrick, *wholeheartedly* forgave his Irish captors and masters.

In fact, he saw his capture and captivity as a purifying period for which he continually gave thanks.

When, years later, his mission to spread Christianity among the Irish was enjoying considerable success, Patrick suffered a severe blow. He was criticised and censured by a gathering of British bishops and called to account for himself. This was the event that fired Patrick into writing his *Confession*:

> *'I was put to the test by a number of my senior fellow-bishops who came to cast up my sins at me in order to discredit my hard work as bishop of this mission ... After thirty years they discovered against me a confession which I had made before I became a deacon ... I confided to my dearest friend what I had done in my boyhood ... God knows – I don't – whether I was yet fifteen.' (26-27)*

This betrayal by someone whom he had considered to be his dearest friend cut Patrick to the core. By exposing this sin of his youth and publicly humiliating him, his enemies had hoped to discredit all his missionary achievements in Ireland. Patrick felt the disgrace of his betrayal and subsequent censure so keenly that he was tempted to abandon his work.

In this, his hour of deepest need, help came directly from God in a dream. The divine vision and its accompanying message gave Patrick the support and encouragement he needed to persevere in his calling and stay with the Irish mission.

We do not know the nature of Patrick's sin but he never defended himself. Neither did he condemn his friend and confidante who betrayed him. On the contrary, he was filled with compassion for him.

> *'My only sorrow ... is for my dearest friend. To him I had confided my very soul ... how did it occur to him afterwards to let me down publicly?' (32)*

In reading the *Confession*, we come to realise that this document is a personal record of Patrick's prayer relationship with God. It is also a documented account of how the Christian teaching on forgiveness was heard and practised by one person. For Patrick was gifted by God with an extraordinary ability to forgive. He forgave totally without holding on to any cancerous residue. Neither his pagan captors, his slave-masters, the hostile bishops nor his close friend are condemned by him. Nor is there any trace of bitterness, resentment or vindictiveness in the document.

Patrick's ability and willingness to forgive is what enabled Almighty God to heal past hurts.

How relevant is St Patrick in today's world? Perhaps the question should be 'How relevant is forgiveness in today's world?' Which one of us can truthfully say that we have nothing and nobody to forgive? That we hold no hurts? That we nourish no feelings of bitterness? The Divine imperative remains with us today as it did in St Patrick's time, 'Forgive us our trespasses as we forgive those who trespass against us.'

Kidnappings, killings, betrayals, abuse and public humiliations are all part of today's experience for many of us. Misunderstandings and divisions are part of the human condition from which we cannot escape. In times of difficulty, it might be encouraging to recall the example of Patrick who forgave totally.

The Far East

Quotations from *Patrick in his own words* by Joseph Duffy.

QUESTIONS

1. Using examples taken from the life of Patrick, show how he *suffered at the hands of others*.
2. What was Patrick's initial reaction to this captivity?
3. How did he eventually come to regard his years in captivity?
4. What event publicly humiliated Patrick?
5. How did Patrick react to this humiliation?
6. Why does the author say that *Patrick was gifted by God with an extraordinary ability to forgive*?

The Importance of Jesus

Christians believe that God sent his only Son, Jesus, to liberate (i.e. free) human beings from the power of sin.

Jesus announced the forgiveness of sins and demonstrated his power over all the bad effects of sin in our world, such as disease, loneliness and starvation.

Consider the following examples:

■ *John* 9:1-38, where Jesus gave sight to a man born blind.
■ *John* 8:1-11, where Jesus lifted the burden of sin from a woman, enabling her to rediscover her self-respect and live her life as God intended.

The Transfiguration by Savoldo ➡

In the book of *Genesis* we are told that the punishment for original sin is *death*. Sin and death are intimately linked together.

By his resurrection Jesus defeated sin and death. Life is not pointless, death is *not* the end. All human beings are invited to share eternal life with God.

Jesus has shown us that it is not a waste of time trying to do good and avoid evil. Making good moral decisions has a great meaning and significance for both our own lives and those around us, in this life and in the life after death.

QUESTIONS

1. Why does the Old Testament book of *Genesis* say about death?
2. Why do Christians believe that the resurrection of Jesus is important?

The Sacrament of Reconciliation

The sacrament of reconciliation celebrates the loving forgiveness of God.

The ceremony for individual confession consists of the following:

- **Confession**

  The penitent (i.e. the person seeking forgiveness) declares his/her sorrow for sins he/she has committed and admits responsibility to the priest who is the representative of the Church.

- **Penance**

  The penitent must be prepared to make up for what he/she has done. Penance may be a prayer or an act designed to help the person overcome his/her selfishness, such as helping care for an elderly relative.

■ **Act of Contrition**
This is a formal prayer said by the penitent which expresses his/her sorrow and a firm commitment not to sin again.

■ **Absolution**
The priest says: *I absolve you of your sins in the name of the Father, and of the Son, and of the Holy Spirit. Amen.*

The sacrament of reconciliation is so called because it *reconciles* people with God and with each other. It expresses the belief that through the power of God's Holy Spirit and the actions of the priest, forgiveness of sins may be given. It reminds Christians that they can return God's love by living good lives.

QUESTIONS

1. What is a *penitent*?
2. Why is the sacrament of *reconciliation* known by that title?
3. What is the purpose of requiring a person to do *penance*?

Working for Peace and Reconciliation

Roger Schutz
▼

There are many groups of Christians across the world who have dedicated their lives to promoting forgiveness and healing in their communities:

■ **The Taizé Community in France**
This community was founded in 1940 by Roger Schutz. It is a monastic community, which consists of both Catholics and Protestants. It has worked tirelessly to heal the wounds of past European conflicts.

■ **The Corrymeela Community in Northern Ireland**

This community was founded in 1965 by Catholics and Protestants. Its aim is to reduce religious conflict and build bridges of peace and reconciliation between the two religious traditions, by bringing Catholics and Protestants together in Christian fellowship.

JOURNAL WORK

Find out about the work of such communities as Taizé or Corrymeela.

CHAPTER TEN

THE DIGNITY OF THE HUMAN PERSON

Introduction

Before exploring the question of human rights, we must first be clear about what it *means* to be human and *why* human rights should be *respected*.

Human Beings are Unique

There are clear and striking *differences* between human beings and all other creatures on our planet.

Consider the following:

■ A chimpanzee can use a stick to probe an anthill for food or to defend himself against attack. However, humans are the only creatures that can take natural materials like iron, stone and wood and turn them into machines, houses and furniture.

This human capacity to *design* and *make* things is without parallel in the animal kingdom. It has allowed people to change the face of the Earth with massive construction projects. Astronauts can even spot the Great Wall of China from their orbit high above our planet.

■ Animals cannot tell stories, compose music, paint pictures nor can they share jokes. Only humans are capable of such things. Birds do not truly sing nor do hyenas really laugh. It is *humans* who hear music in the sound of the thrush and laughter in the hyena's cackle.

■ Animals act on *instinct*, i.e. patterns of behaviour which they have inherited biologically from their ancestors.

For example, a squirrel stores food for the winter but he/she is guided by instinct rather than any freely chosen plan. A squirrel cannot change his/her way of behaving any more than an ant can resign from its community and set up a home on its own.

■ In contrast, human beings are *not* completely dominated by their instincts. People can *learn* from their own experiences and those of others. They can *evaluate* their actions and distinguish between good and evil. People can form their own *plans* for the future and make their own *choices* about how to live their lives.

This is called *free will*. It is the most important difference between humans and all other creatures on Earth. As far as science can tell, animals are not capable of making their own plans for the future nor can animals make decisions about the rightness or wrongness of certain actions.

For example, a dog can be trained to bark and growl at a burglar, but the dog could not work out why stealing is wrong nor could he choose to change sides and become the burglar's assistant.

Human Life is Sacred

We can see that there are significant differences between humans and animals. Human beings are capable of thinking and behaving at an altogether higher level than any other creatures on Earth. *Human life is a different kind of thing from animal life*.

In common with Judaism and Islam, Christianity teaches that human beings are completely *unique* creatures. Christians believe that:

■ Humans have not evolved to live as we do by blind chance. Rather,

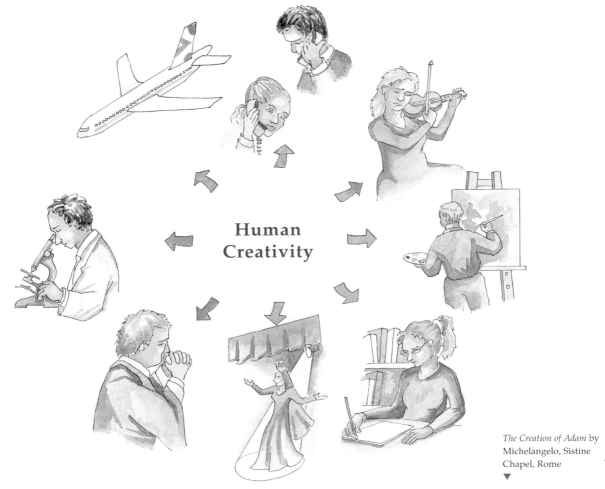

Human Creativity

The Creation of Adam by Michelangelo, Sistine Chapel, Rome

humans are only capable of thinking and acting freely in our special way because God has given us the capacity to do so.

- Women and men are made in God's own *image and likeness* (*Genesis* 1:26). This is because, alone among the creatures of the Earth, human beings have been given the gifts of *reason* and *free will*.

- All people are God's children. Each person is unique and unrepeatable. Everyone is immensely valuable to God.

Each human being has a unique dignity that should be *respected* and *protected*. This is what Christians mean when they say that *human life is sacred*.

QUESTIONS

1. Use the words provided in the box below to fill in the spaces in the following extract.

   - learn ■ instinct ■ cannot ■ make ■ not ■ evaluate
   - own ■ design ■ differences ■ compose ■ humans
   - choices ■ jokes

   The human capacity to _____ and _____ things is without parallel in the animal kingdom.

   Animals _____ tell stories, _____ music, paint pictures or share _____. Only _____ are capable of such things.

   Animals act on _____. In contrast, humans are _____ completely dominated by their instincts. People can _____ from experience. They can _____ their actions and distinguish between good and evil. People can make their _____ plans for the future and make free _____ about how to live their lives.

   We can see that there are significant _____ between humans and animals.

2. State two important differences between human beings and all the other creatures on Earth.

3. Explain why Christianity teaches that

   Women and men are made in God's own image and likeness.

4. What do Christians mean when they say that *human life is sacred*?

The Universal Declaration

The UN General
Assembly in
New York ➡

In 1948, the General Assembly of the United Nations issued its *Universal Declaration of Human Rights*.

Human Rights may be defined as

> *Those basic entitlements which each person needs to promote and defend his/her freedom and dignity.*

The thirty articles of the *Universal Declaration* set out the standards which all United Nations' member countries agreed every nation should try to meet. These articles are summarised below.

Every human being is entitled to:

❖ Life.

❖ Liberty and security of person.

❖ Not be made a slave.

❖ Not be physically, psychologically or sexually abused.

❖ Protection by the law.

❖ A fair and public hearing in the courts, i.e. be presumed innocent until proven guilty.

❖ Freedom of movement and residence.

❖ Marry and found a family.

❖ Own property.

❖ Freedom of conscience and religion.

❖ Freedom of opinion and expression.

❖ Freedom of peaceful assembly and of association.

❖ Seek and receive information and ideas.

❖ Education.

❖ Take part in politics.

❖ Work.

❖ Fair wages and equal pay for equal work.

❖ Social security.

❖ A decent standard of living.

❖ Join a trade union.

❖ Rest and leisure.

All these rights are to be upheld, irrespective of any differences of race, colour, sex, language, religion, political opinion, social origin, property or birth.

QUESTIONS

1. Explain what is meant by *human rights*.
2. Which organisation issued the Universal Declaration of Human Rights in 1948?
3. Read the following statement:

   Human rights are fundamental to our nature. Without them we cannot live as human beings.

   Then choose any *four* of the rights listed above and, in each case, explain why they are said to be important.

The Abuse of Human Rights

Sadly, abuses of human rights go on despite the *UN Declaration*. When this important document was approved by the UN's member states, they did not insist that, if any country failed to uphold these rights, it would be expelled. As a result, many of the UN's members only pay lip-service to the protection of human rights. Many people are left at the mercy of governments with scant respect for human life. Consider the use of *torture*, namely,

> *the infliction of severe pain, especially as a punishment or means of persuasion.*

Torture is prohibited by all international human rights' treaties. Yet, reports from human rights' campaigners claim that it is used by the security forces of more than eighty countries today.

QUESTIONS

1. Identify one serious weakness of the *UN Declaration on Human Rights*.

2. Read the following story by a survivor of a Nazi concentration camp:

   First they came for the Jews
   and I did not speak out –
   because I was not a Jew.

   Then they came for the trade unionists
   and I did not speak out –
   because I was not a trade unionist.

   Then they came for me –
   and there was no one left
   to speak out for me.

   What point does the author make about the importance of protecting the human rights of all people in both one's *own* society and those *elsewhere*?

Christians and the Defence of Human Rights

During his earthly ministry, Jesus always showed deep concern and respect for the needs of others:

- Jesus noticed the widow giving coins in the temple (*Mark* 12:41-44).
- Jesus cured the woman who touched the hem of his robe (*Mark* 5:25-34).
- Jesus was kind to the sinful woman who anointed his feet (*Luke* 7:36-50).
- Jesus cured the disturbed man who had been forced to live among the tombs (*Mark* 5:1-20).
- Jesus cured Bartimaeus who had been forced to beg because he was blind (*Mark* 10:46-52).

CONSIDER JESUS..

IN EGYPT:
A refugee from despotic government
IN GALILEE:
The travelling miracle worker who healed the sick, fed the hungry.
ON THE HILLSIDE:
The teacher who urged his disciples to care for the poor, the sick and the imprisoned.
IN JERUSALEM:
The prophet, persecuted by the political and religious establishment.
IN COURT:
The prisoner of conscience convicted on false testimony.
ON GOLGOTHA:
The martyr of an occupying colonial power.
RISEN AND ASCENDED:
The Saviour of the whole world.

HUMAN RIGHTS IS A CHRISTIAN CONCERN

Jesus made it clear that people show their love for God by loving their fellow human beings. This is a real *challenge*. Too many people find it easier to say, '*It's none of my business*'. Christians are called to respect the rights of each person and do all that they can to protect them.

QUESTIONS

At the Second Vatican Council, the assembled leaders of the Catholic Church declared that:

> *A special obligation binds us to make ourselves the neighbour of every person ... whether he/she is an old person abandoned by all, a refugee or a hungry person who disturbs our conscience.*

1. Identify the *three* groups of people mentioned who need help in defence of their basic human rights.
2. Explain what it means to make oneself the *neighbour* of people in need. Give practical examples of how they might be helped.

Profile: Oscar Romero, Champion of the Rights of the Poor

Oscar Romero is one of the great Christian martyrs of modern times. When Oscar Romero was made an archbishop in 1977, El Salvador was one of the poorest countries in Central America, and was gripped by a terrible civil war. The military regime and its death squads, tools of the small number of powerful families who controlled ninety per cent of the country's wealth, were systematically murdering those who campaigned for justice, democracy and human rights. Thousands of people were killed, including many priests, missionaries and lay workers.

At the time of his appointment, Oscar Romero was seen by many as a friend of the people in power, someone who would not rock the boat. But rock the boat is precisely what Oscar Romero did. He placed the Church firmly on the side of the oppressed. He challenged those in authority to face up to the injustice they were causing and to make amends. He offered support and comfort to his suffering people by his words and actions. All this was too much for those in authority. Romero had become dangerous, subversive and a troublemaker, someone who had to be eliminated. On 24 March 1980, as he celebrated Mass in a city convent, Oscar Romero was murdered, shot through the heart by an assassin.

Even though Romero knew his life was in danger, he was not prepared to compromise the Gospel message.

Many people consider Romero to be a martyr, because he faithfully followed the example of Jesus even to the point of giving his life for him.

The Sunday Message

QUESTIONS

1. Who was Oscar Romero?
2. Describe the conditions in El Salvador between 1977 and 1980.
3. What did many people think of Oscar Romero at the time he was first appointed archbishop?
4. What kind of things did Oscar Romero do after his appointment to anger those in power?
5. How was Oscar Romero killed?
6. Why do many Christians consider Oscar Romero to be a *martyr*?

JOURNAL WORK

Christianity teaches that

> *Faith, if it does not lead to action is, in itself, a lifeless thing.*
> *James 2:17*

Why should Christians become involved in voluntary organisations which campaign to protect human rights?

CHAPTER ELEVEN

LAW AND MORALITY

Introduction

On First Avenue at Forty-Sixth Street in New York City stands a massive building of glass and marble. It is the headquarters of the United Nations Organisation. Outside it flutter the flags of its member states. We may define a *state* as

> *a community of people organised under a government.*

The Role of the State

Christians and non-Christians agree that the state has a duty to maintain peace and order among its citizens. The state does so by setting out *laws* and insisting on its citizens obeying them.

Law

The figure of Justice, Dublin Castle ▼

We may define *law* as

> *a rule set out by the state authorities, which its citizens are obliged to obey.*

All laws should be designed to uphold the *common good*, i.e. to protect the rights of all members of a society and achieve justice for them.

For example, *freedom of speech* is a fundamental right that every state should protect in its laws.

> *Everyone has the right to freedom of opinion and expression; this right includes freedom to hold opinions without interference and to seek, receive*

*and impart information and ideas through any media and regardless of
frontiers.*

Article 19, *Declaration of Human Rights*

Freedom of speech is
a right to cherish,
defend and use
responsibly. ➡

In a democracy, people are free to think and speak as they choose. However,
people do *not* have an unlimited freedom of speech. The law of the state
imposes certain *limits* on the freedom of speech in order to uphold the
common good.

For example, the following are against the law:

■ Making false statements about someone which damages his/her
reputation. When written this is called *libel* and when spoken it is called
slander.

■ Using abusive or threatening language or behaviour intended to incite
racial or religious hatred.

QUESTIONS

1. Explain the following terms:

(a) *state*, (b) *law*, (c) *upholding the common good*.

2. What is meant by *freedom of speech*?

3. Give two examples where it might be necessary to *limit* the freedom
of speech in the interest of the common good.

Obeying the Law

It is important to distinguish between *law* and *morality*. Generally speaking, people are obliged to obey the law of the land. Where an illegal act is committed, i.e. the law is broken, the person who has done so is held responsible and, if caught, will be put on trial. If found guilty, he/she will be punished.

However, simply because a law of the state says that certain behaviour is unacceptable does *not* automatically make it morally wrong.

For example, a person may be obliged by the law to join his/her country's armed forces in time of war. However, he/she would be *morally* obliged to refuse military service if he/she was a committed pacifist, e.g. members of the Society of Friends are opposed to all forms of violence.

Some people think that the law of the state should be the *only* standard by which people decide what is right and what is wrong. However, the law can sometimes be used to *deprive* people of something to which they are rightfully entitled. What is legal may *not* necessarily be moral. Consider the following example:

Case Study – Apartheid

Apartheid was a system of segregation (i.e. dividing people) that came into operation in South Africa with the Population Registration Act of 1948. Every citizen was given a racial label – white, coloured, Asian, Chinese or black – and each black person was classified according to tribe.

Every inch of the country was divided into segregated districts, and it became illegal (i.e. against the law) for non-white persons to live or work outside their allocated areas.

More than 3.5 million people lost their homes and businesses through the Group Areas Act of 1950, which allowed the whites to take possession of the prime residential and business areas and to set up a system of racially segregated transportation, education, leisure facilities, and even public toilets. Some jobs were advertised as being 'for whites only'.

The movement of black people between the areas was controlled by the notorious Pass Laws. Black workers had to carry a pass at all times and would be allowed, or refused entry, in to a district only after showing this document. The most serious restrictions on freedom came in 1956, when black and coloured voters were removed from the electoral rolls.

By 1969 the South African government had passed a series of laws enabling it to suppress all criticism of its racial policies. The police could arrest and detain citizens without trial, withholding their right to see a lawyer and prohibiting them access to their own families.

This catalogue of pro-white, anti-black legislation created an atmosphere in which violent protest became inevitable. A long, hard struggle was fought before civil rights for all citizens were reinstated in the 1990s.

Frank McLynn, *Famous Trials: Cases That Made History*

QUESTIONS

1. What is meant by an illegal act?
2. Give an example of where a person might believe that disobeying the law of the state is the morally correct thing to do.
3. Consider the South African experience of *Apartheid*. What does it say about the view that the law of the state should be the only standard by which people decide what is right and what is wrong. Give two examples from the above extract to support your answer.

Law and Morality

Christians believe that people should respect and obey the laws of the state, but they should *not* do so blindly. People are *only* obliged to obey a law if it is morally right to do so. Jesus said:

> *Render to Caesar the things that are Caesar's; and to God the things that are God's.*
> *Luke* 20:25

Christians believe that the state does not have the final say as to what is right and what is wrong. There is a *higher* standard, which is *not* set by human beings. It is for this reason that the Catholic Church teaches:

> *God's law continues to bind no matter what the civil (i.e. state) law says.*
> *Love is for Life*

A person must remember this when making a moral decision.

Christians believe that people should obey the law of the state as long as it upholds the common good. If there is a conflict between what God wants and what the state demands, then a person must do what is right, even if it means breaking the law.

The *Acts of the Apostles* tells of how Peter was arrested and brought before the Sanhedrin. The High Priest ordered Peter to stop preaching about Jesus. Peter replied:

> *Obedience to God comes before obedience to men.*
> *Acts* 5:29

To do the right thing demands great *courage*. Courage has been defined as

> *the ability to make a moral choice, even if it is in opposition to other people who have power over you.*

To courageously follow one's conscience in opposition to the abuse of state power can cost a person his/her life. Consider the story of Franz Jagerstatter's opposition to the Nazis.

Profile: Franz Jagerstatter

Franz was a farmer, married with three young daughters, in rural Austria. He had been a typical fun-loving young man who underwent a profound conversion to Catholicism about the time of this marriage in 1936. Then, in 1938, the Nazis occupied Austria and united it with Germany.

Hitler held a ballot afterwards to justify his action. Franz was the *only person* in his village of St. Radegund to vote against the Nazi occupation of Austria.

When World War Two began the following year, Franz refused to join the German armed forces. He announced that he would not support a tyrant such as Hitler by fighting in his army, even though the law required it. He also refused the offer to be assigned to non-combat duties.

All the time Franz was put under enormous pressure from the authorities. They told him that he had a duty to obey the call to fight for his country. It was said that he was failing to defend his wife and children.

Franz disagreed. He believed that Hitler's war was utterly unjustified and causing horrific loss of life.

Eventually, Franz was conscripted by law into the army. However, he refused to take the oath of service. He was tried by a military court and sentenced to death. He was beheaded on 9 August 1943.

Franz Jagerstatter was willing to die rather than fight for Hitler. He was put to death for obeying his conscience and refusing to accept the abuse of state power.

QUESTIONS

1. Explain Christian teaching about when it is morally right to obey the law of the state.

2. What is *courage*?

3. Why did Franz Jagerstatter refuse to accept the law requiring him to fight in Hitler's army?

4. Do you think that (a) Franz Jaggerstatter was correct *or* (b) he went too far in his protest against the Nazis? Explain your answer.

Law in Islam

The ideal Muslim society is a *theocracy*, i.e. where a state is governed by laws based on the teachings of Islam.

Over the centuries, Islamic leaders and scholars have compiled an all-embracing code of morality and law called the *Shari'a*. All Muslims are expected to faithfully observe the *Shari'a*. This is why in most countries with an Islamic majority, the following things are forbidden and punishable by the law of the state:

- Adultery.
- Consumption of alcohol.
- Astrology.
- Gambling.
- Use of unprescribed drugs.
- Prostitution.
- Dancing between men and women.

Muslims strongly defend the *Shari'a* against the charge that it is too harsh. They point out that:

- Statistics for crime and violence are much *lower*, in Islamic countries than in non-Islamic ones.
- Non-Muslims living in a Muslim state do *not* have to become Muslims. However, they must abide by Islamic law.

QUESTIONS

1. What is a *theocracy*?
2. What is the *Shari'a*?
3. Identify three things forbidden and punishable according to the *Shari'a*.
4. How do Muslims respond to the claim that the *Shari'a* is unnecessarily harsh?

Part Two

Exploring Issues

CHAPTER TWELVE

ABORTION

Life Before Birth

The Medical Facts

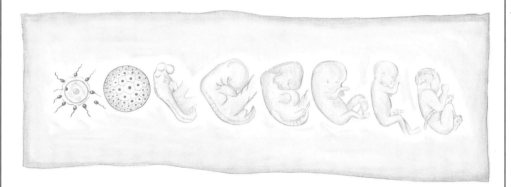

The development
of the unborn child

Day 1	*Conception* occurs. A male sex cell (the *sperm*) fertilises a female sex cell (the *ovum*) after sexual intercourse. The sperm and ovum unite to form an *embryo*. The person's genetic make up is complete. Colour of eyes, sex (i.e. whether male or female), fingerprints and even build (i.e. slim, tall, etc.) are decided. A unique individual is created.
Day 23	Heart begins to beat regularly and the foundations for the nervous system have been laid down.
Day 28	Legs, arms, eyes and ears begin to form.
Week 6	Skeleton complete and muscle reflexes are present. Liver, kidneys and lungs formed. Electrical brain-wave patterns can be detected and recorded.

Week 8	→	All organs functioning. Milk teeth formed, as are fingers, thumbs, ankles and toes. From the end of the eighth week the unborn child is known as a *foetus*.
Week 10	→	Sensitive to touch. Can turn his/her head, bend elbows and wrists independently.
Week 12	→	Capable of swallowing. Fingernails begin to develop. Vocal chords complete.
Week 16	→	Half his/her birth weight.
Week 20	→	Hair, eyebrows and eyelashes appear. Can turn body, kick and suck thumb. Responds to stimuli (e.g. noise) from outside the womb.
Week 28	→	Eyes open. Can hear mother's heartbeat.
Weeks 36-40	→	Baby approaches birth.

QUESTIONS

1. What is *conception*?
2. When is the unborn child known as (a) an *embryo* and (b) a *foetus*?
3. Match the information in column *B* with the time given in column *A*.

A	B
Day 23	Baby responds to stimuli (i.e. noises) from outside the womb.
Week 6	All organs functioning. Milk teeth formed as are fingers, thumbs, ankles and toes.
Week 8	Heart begins to beat regularly and foundations for the nervous system have been laid down.
Week 20	Skeleton complete and muscle reflexes present. Liver, kidneys and lungs formed. Electrical brain-wave patterns can be recorded.

Abortion

An *abortion** may be defined as

> *any procedure that deliberately terminates a pregnancy and causes the death of an unborn child.*

In an abortion, the embryo or foetus is removed from the womb usually *before* he/she is capable of life independent from his/her mother.

The methods used to carry out an abortion may involve the use of either *surgery or drugs*, or a combination of *both*, depending on the stage the mother's pregnancy has reached.

An abortion must be distinguished from a *miscarriage*, i.e. where an embryo/foetus is *spontaneously* expelled from the mother's womb *without* any outside intervention.

---

* Also referred to as a *direct* abortion or a *procured* abortion.

Reasons for Abortion

- For some women an abortion seems to offer the best solution to a distressing personal problem, especially in cases of pregnancy due to rape or incest.

- Sometimes economic hardship and/or pregnancy late in married life may lead some women to believe that an abortion provides the only solution to their problems.

- In some cases, powerful pressure is applied to the pregnant woman by another interested party. This can be the father of the unborn child, her relatives, or perhaps someone from whom she may seek advice.

- Sometimes a pregnancy may be unwelcome if the parents believe that there is a high risk of their child being born with a disability. They may opt for an abortion out of fear about the future.

- Some women become pregnant without being married or in a stable relationship. People are not always understanding or sympathetic to single mothers.

Some of these mothers are very young. They may be lonely, confused, fearful of the future and vulnerable. They may opt for an abortion out of fear or confusion and bitterly regret this decision later.

QUESTIONS

1. What is meant by the term *abortion*?
2. Identify *three* reasons why women sometimes choose to have an abortion.

The Morality of Abortion

Although abortion is legal in many countries today, the Catholic Church and most of the other Christian Churches have always taught that abortion is morally wrong. However, the belief that abortion is unjustifiable pre-dates Christianity. The *Hippocratic Oath* sworn by Greek doctors from the sixth century B.C. onwards stated:

I will neither give a deadly drug to anybody if asked for it, nor will I make a suggestion to this effect. Similarly, I will not give a woman an abortive remedy.

The early Christian collection entitled *the Didache* (i.e. *the Teaching of the Twelve Apostles*), written in the early second century, taught:

You shall not kill the embryo by abortion nor cause the newborn child to perish.

The Catholic Church opposes abortion. It teaches that:

■ Human life begins at *conception*. Advances in medical knowledge support this belief.

> *It is scientifically correct to say that an individual human life begins at conception, when the egg and sperm join to form the embryo, and that this developing human always is a member of our species in all stages of its life.*
> Dr Micheline Matthews Roth, Harvard University Medical School, USA

■ As a member of the human race, the embryo/foetus is entitled to the *respect* due to any person. Abortion denies him/her the most *basic* of all human rights – the right to life itself.

■ Abortion violates the fifth commandment. Human life is *sacred*. Each person's life is a gift from God, which should be protected from the moment of conception until his/her natural death.

Medical Treatment

Since both mother and unborn child are human beings, it is a doctor's duty to regard *both* of them as his/her patients. If a medical crisis arises, the doctor must try to sustain the pregnancy as long as there is a reasonable prospect of saving the lives of both the mother and her unborn child.

The Catholic Church teaches that essential medical treatment should always be given to a pregnant woman, for example chemotherapy for breast cancer, which tragically occurs in an estimated one per thousand pregnancies. This treatment may be given even if it results in the death of the unborn child, *provided* that two *conditions* are met:

(i) the death of the unborn child is *not* a directly intended consequence of the treatment given;

and

(ii) there is *no other* effective way of managing the treatment of the woman successfully.

QUESTIONS

1. What is the Hippocratic Oath?
2. Why does the Catholic Church oppose abortion?
3. Explain the teaching of the Catholic Church regarding treatment of a pregnant woman suffering from cancer.

Where a Woman is a Victim of Rape

Rape is a horrific crime. The victims of rape need support, sympathy and understanding. Many need skilled help, not just immediately, but for a long time after the event to try to heal the emotional damage they have suffered.

The victim of rape has a right to seek medical help with a view to *preventing* conception. This is done by removing the rapist's semen *before* fertilisation occurs. This medical procedure is *not* an abortion because conception has *not* yet happened. The Catholic Church teaches that such action is morally right. It is part of a woman's legitimate resistance to the rapist's attack.

Although pregnancy after rape is *rare*, it does sometimes happen. The Catholic Church teaches that this is a situation which requires great sensitivity, with a careful balance of compassion for the victim and meeting the demands of justice. The child developing in the woman's womb is a new human being. As such, his/her life must be protected. This child is not responsible for what has happened. The child cannot rightly be made to pay with his/her life for the man's crime in violating the woman.

QUESTIONS

1. What medical treatment should a victim of rape seek as soon as possible after suffering such a horrific crime?
2. Why does the Catholic Church oppose abortion in the case of a woman made pregnant as a result of rape?

The Threat of Suicide

Studies* show that:

■ Suicide in pregnancy is a rare event.

■ Suicide is more common in the *post-delivery period*, i.e. after the baby is born.

■ Women are more likely to commit suicide after an abortion than during pregnancy.

A threat of suicide by a pregnant woman is a desperate cry for help. There are people willing to answer this call.

Sources*:

(1) *Green Paper on Abortion*, Govt. Publications, 1999.

(2) L. Appleby, 'Suicide During Pregnancy', *British Medical Journal*, Vol. 30, 1991.

CURA

CURA is a national network of support funded largely from the resources of the Irish Catholic Church with a grant from the Department of Health.

CURA offers information, advice and counselling to any woman, married or single, faced with the dilemma of an unwanted pregnancy.

CURA's experienced counsellors seek to help a woman explore the various options and reach an informed decision about her pregnancy. Help offered includes accommodation and medical treatment, at no expense to the woman herself, during the pregnancy if she is prepared to allow the baby to be born and not aborted.

CURA also offers help to women who have had an abortion, but who have later come to regret doing so.

Contact numbers for CURA's confidential telephone service can be found in local telephone directories.

QUESTIONS

1. What is CURA?
2. Give a brief account of the services it offers a woman facing a crisis pregnancy.

JOURNAL WORK

In each case below, state the consequences of each choice for: (a) the woman, and (b) her child.

A Woman Discovers That She Is Pregnant

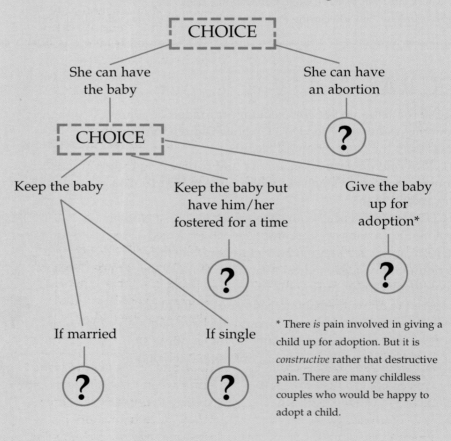

* There *is* pain involved in giving a child up for adoption. But it is *constructive* rather that destructive pain. There are many childless couples who would be happy to adopt a child.

The Arguments For and Against Abortion

FOR	AGAINST
The rights of the mother are at stake. It is her body. She should have the right to choose whether or not to have the baby.	The mother's rights are not denied. Biologically, however, the foetus is *someone else's* body. Abortion deprives another human being of his/her fundamental right to life. Further, there are many childless couples who would gladly *adopt* a child.
Abortion is more a woman's issue than a man's. It is the woman who becomes pregnant, perhaps without her consent.	The responsibility of defending human life rests equally on *all* people, male and female.
A woman facing a crisis pregnancy should be treated with compassion. She should be granted an abortion if she wants it.	Sometimes abortion is sought for serious reasons. However, compassion for one person's distress cannot justify the taking of a child's life.
In some cases, babies are conceived as a result of rape or incest. Such events are tragedies enough in themselves without adding an unwanted child.	Rape and incest are dreadful crimes. However, the fact that an illegal, unwanted act has taken place is *not* sufficient reason for taking a child's life. One action that is wrong should not lead to another that is also wrong.

A severely disabled child may have a poor quality of life and may impose great strains on his/her parents. The parents should be offered the choice of an abortion if tests detect the disability while the child is still in the womb.

If accepted, this argument would imply that a person with a disability is a second class citizen in our society. *A disabled person is a fellow human being*. Who has the right, therefore, to end his/her life?

QUESTION

Examine the arguments for and against abortion.

Which do you find the most convincing – the arguments *for* abortion or the arguments *against* abortion?

Give reasons for your choice.

CHAPTER THIRTEEN

WAR AND PEACE

Introduction

Politics has been defined as

> *the art of solving problems without the use of violence.*

When politics fails, people often turn to violence to settle a dispute. Violence can take many forms, ranging from verbal abuse to physical harm.

War is the most destructive form of physical conflict. Those who respect human life cannot be indifferent to the issue of war.

What is War?

War may be defined as

> *armed hostilities between two groups in which each side puts people forward to fight and kill.*

There have been countless wars throughout human history, usually caused by a number of deep-seated disagreements, which have built up over many years. They are often sparked off by some minor incident.

THE CAUSES OF WAR

1. The desire to overthrow an oppressive and unjust government.
2. The struggle for national independence, i.e. when a people forcibly expel an oppressive *foreign* ruler.
3. The clash of opposing political outlooks, such as between fascism and communism in World War Two.
4. The eruption of racial hatred and/or religious bigotry.
5. The lust for power by an individual or group and the subjugation of a population by force.
6. The fear of a threatening, militaristic neighbour launching a surprise attack.
7. The desire for revenge in order to undo a defeat in a previous conflict.
8. One state's economic ambition to seize the natural resources of another.

Wars and War-Related Deaths, 1500 to 1970

Region	Number of Deaths		
	Civilian	Military	Total
North America	204,000	1,288,000	1,532,000
Latin America	1,932,000	1,088,000	3,239,000
Europe	48,935,000	44,119,000	93,450,000
Middle East	464,000	709,000	1,235,000
South Asia	2,302,000	1,171,000	3,610,000
Far East	16,513,000	13,398,000	31,185,000
Oceania	50,000	137,000	187,000
Sub-Saharan Africa	4,806,000	1,597,000	6,625,000
Other Africa	442,000	202,000	644,000
Total	75,649,000	63,709,000	141,901,000

Note: These figures are incomplete, the breakdown of civilian and military deaths is not available in all cases. Based upon the research of Dr William Eckhardt, Lentz Peace Research Laboratory, and published in *World Military and Social Expenditure* (ed. Ruth Sivard, 1991), Stockholm International Peace Research Institute.

Source: *Irish Times*, 5 May 1998.

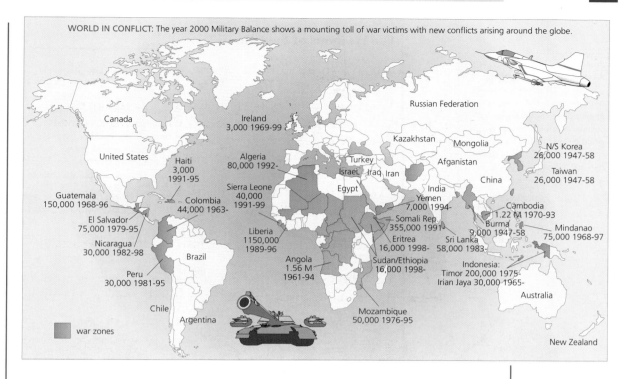

WORLD IN CONFLICT: The year 2000 Military Balance shows a mounting toll of war victims with new conflicts arising around the globe.

The Cost of War

■ Loss of life.

■ Physical and mental suffering of the survivors.

■ A refugee crisis.

■ Destruction of property.

■ Enormous debt.

QUESTIONS

1. What is *war*?

2. Read the following statements. In each case state whether you agree or disagree with them. Give reasons for your answers.

   (a) *All wars are caused by power-hungry individuals. If Hitler had not existed, the Second World War would never have taken place.*

   (b) *People's greed, their desire for material wealth, land and possessions — this is at the root of many wars.*

   (c) *War, conflict and violence are a part of human nature. Humans are naturally aggressive creatures. Thus, war can never be completely eliminated.*

3. In what ways do people suffer in wars?

The Weapons of the Future

Propaganda
A country's TV and radio can already be subject to broadcasts of propaganda, but morphed images of an enemy leader will soon be possible. For instance, he could be seen telling his own troops to surrender on his own national TV network.

Bombs
A suitcase-size electromagnetic-pulse bomb could be placed by undercover troops next to an enemy's central bank. When detonated, electronic devices in the building would be burnt out by a high-powered pulse, causing financial chaos.

Logic Bombs
Communications systems could be shut down by computer 'logic' bombs detonated nearby. They would scramble air-traffic control computers to re-route aircraft carrying military supplies while goods trains would be sent to wrong destinations.

Microbes
Specially bred microbes that feed on electronic software and cabling could be secretly fed into the switching systems of telephone and computer networks. They would cause widespread disruption by linking up with viruses.

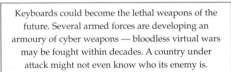

Keyboards could become the lethal weapons of the future. Several armed forces are developing an armoury of cyber weapons — bloodless virtual wars may be fought within decades. A country under attack might not even know who its enemy is.

Intelligence
Thousands of tiny sensors could be scattered on enemy territory to observe military movements. Chemicals could be put in food supplies to track troops by detecting their breath or sweat.

The Just War Theory

One influential Christian response to the awful reality of war is known as the *just war* theory. It was developed by two Christian saints, Augustine and Thomas Aquinas. It acknowledges that as an individual person has a right to self-defence, so too must a community or state have the right to protect itself when its basic rights are threatened.

The just war theory aims to:

- identify those conditions whereby a community/state would be morally justified in going to war;

  and

- put restraints on how people conduct the war so as to limit the harm inflicted.

Augustine and Thomas Aquinas held that moral standards applied in wartime just as they do in peacetime. They set out the just war theory to provide guidance to people when making the difficult decisions that have to be made about war. However, even if all the conditions for a war to be termed *just* are met, this in *no way* means that war is ever to be considered either desirable or good.

Indeed, war is usually the result of failures on *both* sides and it is *rare* that one side is entirely right and the other side entirely wrong. We shall now examine the conditions for a just war.

Conditions for a Just War

1 Just Cause

The war must be one of defence against an unprovoked attack (see article 13 of the UN Charter).

2 Right Intention

The aim of those going to war must be to restore peace and achieve reconciliation. It must not be an act of revenge.

3 Last Resort

All other ways must be explored before going to war. All negotiations must be tried and have failed, and all peaceful alternatives must be exhausted.

4 Likelihood of Success

There must be a reasonable hope that the objectives for which the war is fought can be achieved. If a country is hopelessly out-gunned by the aggressor (i.e. the attacking side) and has no chance of victory, then the harm caused by war could be greater than that caused by surrender.

5 Principle of Proportion

The war should not inflict more suffering than would be experienced by *not* going to war.

6 Safety of Non-Combatants

Civilians should never be the intended targets of the war. Nothing can justify the indiscriminate killing of civil populations.

QUESTIONS

1. Name the two Christian thinkers who set out the *just war* theory?
2. List the six conditions for a just war.
3. Consider the following situation. In each case explain why they would be *against* the conditions of the just war theory.
   - Refusal to enter into negotiations to prevent war occurring.
   - Attacking an immeasurably more powerful opponent in certain knowledge of one's own defeat.
   - Shooting prisoners of war.
   - Bombing civilian targets such as hospitals in order to demoralise the enemy population.

JOURNAL WORK

Having considered the just war theory, can the use of nuclear weapons in warfare ever by justified?

Give reasons for your answer.

Jihad

Jihad is often understood by non-Muslims to simply mean *a holy war* against those considered to be enemies of Islam. In fact, it has a broader meaning. The word *Jihad* comes from the Arabic phrase

> *jihad fi sabee Allah,*

which means

> *striving in God's cause.*

Jihad can be understood as the duty of every Muslim to:
- be faithful to the teachings of Islam in his/her daily life;
- ensure that its teachings are spread;
- defend Islam against attack.

The front of the Sbarro pizzeria in Jerusalem after a suicide bomb attack by a Palestinian which killed 18 ➡

Jihad *can* take the form of physical violence.

The *Qur'an*, however, forbids Muslims to engage in unprovoked aggression.

> *Fight in the way of Allah, against those who fight against you. But do not begin hostilities. Allah loveth no aggressors.*

Muslims believe that it is their duty to resist any threat to Islam by force, if it becomes necessary either by direct action or by supporting those to carry out acts of violence in the defence of Islam.

QUESTIONS

1. What is the meaning of the Arabic phrase *jihad fi sabee Allah*?
2. What does the *Qur'an* teach Muslims about war?
3. Muslims believe that *jihad* means they must fulfil certain *duties*. What are they?

Pacifism

Christians who accept the just war theory agree that war is always morally wrong whenever those involved *deliberately* commit acts such as:

- murdering non-combatants, i.e. the wounded, children and the aged;
- torturing or executing prisoners;
- cutting off food and water to civilian populations;

■ causing people to die from disease and starvation.

Opponents of the just war theory point out, however, that it is very difficult to avoid causing harm to innocent people in time of war. As a result they reject war of *any* kind.

Those who object out of conscience to all forms of warfare are called *pacifists**. They refuse to fight in wars and try to find other, non-violent ways to solve conflicts between people.

In times of war, some pacifist volunteers do serve as stretcher-bearers and medics in an effort to save lives.

Pacifists use non-violent forms of protest to bring about change. For example:

■ Peaceful demonstrations or sit-ins.

■ Boycotting shops selling rugs made using child labour.

■ Writing letters of protest to newspapers.

*All members of the Society of Friends are pacifists. They are opposed to *all* forms of violence.

COMMENT

Those Christians who believe that war is sometimes tragically necessary or unavoidable *never* accept it as a good thing. Human life can only flourish where there is *peace*.

Profile: Mahatma Gandhi

One of the most famous pacifists of modern times was Mohandas K. Gandhi (1869-1948). He was a great Hindu holy man and teacher who became known as *the Mahatma* (meaning *great soul*). He was also leader of the nationalist movement that sought India's independence from Britain.

Gandhi developed *satyagraha* (meaning *steadfastness in truth*). This was the theory and practice of non-violent resistance. He believed that the refusal to retaliate or to use any form of violence would eventually defeat any opponent, though it would demand great self-sacrifice and suffering.

In 1920, Gandhi became leader of the Indian National Congress, which adopted a policy of non-co-operation with the British administration. He led protest marches against unjust British policies (such as the 1930 tax on salt) and encouraged boycotting British goods (especially clothing). Gandhi was imprisoned on many occasions.

Eventually, India gained its independence from Britain in 1947. Tragically, Gandhi was assassinated by a Hindu extremist on 30 January 1948.

QUESTIONS

1. What does it mean to be a *pacifist*?
2. Why do some people become pacifists?
3. How do some pacifists help reduce people's suffering in time of war?
4. Explain the meaning of *non-violent protest*.
5. What is the meaning of Gandhi's title *the Mahatma*? Why do you think he was he given it by the Indian people?
6. What is *satyagraha*?

PROJECT

Find out about the work of the International Movement of the Red Cross and the Red Crescent.

Peace

War breaks out when the conditions for peaceful co-existence breakdown. These conditions are:

1. Clear, mutually acceptable territorial boundaries between states.
2. Adequate food and natural resources.
3. Mutual tolerance of differences and economic co-operation.
4. A form of government which is both accepted by and accountable to the people of the state.

Prejudice

A Canadian social researcher wrote letters in response to a hundred holiday advertisements. In each case he asked the hotel manager to reserve a room for him. He wrote two letters to each hotel, looking for a room on identical dates but using a different name on each letter. One name was obviously *Jewish*, while the other was not.

Ninety-nine per cent of the hotels offered the non-Jewish enquirer accommodation, but the Jewish enquirer was only offered accommodation in thirty-six per cent of the same hotels.

Why did almost two-thirds of the hotels' management react so negatively to the request for a room from the 'Jewish' enquirer? The answer is that they were *prejudiced*. We may define prejudice as

> *the act of making up one's mind before finding out the facts and reaching a decision without good reasons to support it.*

A deeply prejudiced person is one who refuses to change his/her views even when confronted with the truth.

A fair-minded person does not reach a decision about someone or something until *after* considering the facts.

It is often only when one has been on the receiving end of prejudice that one comes to realise how unfair it is and how much harm it can cause.

Discrimination

Wherever people are treated badly or unfairly simply because others are prejudiced against them, it is said that these people are victims of *discrimination*.

People are usually discriminated against on grounds that they belong to a particular:

- race
- religion
- gender (usually female)
- age (especially the elderly)
- disability (physical or mental).

Refugees

According to the Geneva Convention (1951) a refugee is defined as

> *a person who, due to a well-founded fear of being persecuted for reasons of race, religion, nationality or politics, is living outside the country of*

his/her origin and is unable, or because of fears for his/her safety, unwilling to return there.

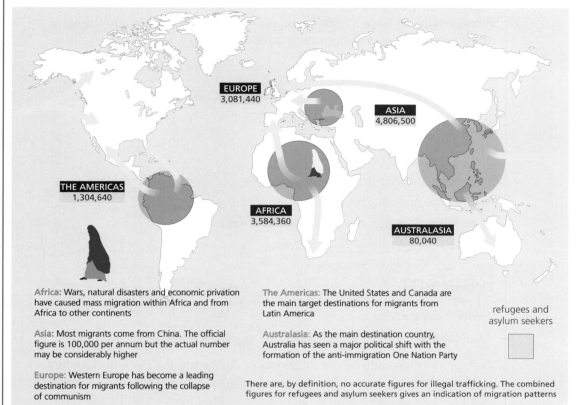

EUROPE
3,081,440

ASIA
4,806,500

THE AMERICAS
1,304,640

AFRICA
3,584,360

AUSTRALASIA
80,040

Africa: Wars, natural disasters and economic privation have caused mass migration within Africa and from Africa to other continents

Asia: Most migrants come from China. The official figure is 100,000 per annum but the actual number may be considerably higher

Europe: Western Europe has become a leading destination for migrants following the collapse of communism

The Americas: The United States and Canada are the main target destinations for migrants from Latin America

Australasia: As the main destination country, Australia has seen a major political shift with the formation of the anti-immigration One Nation Party

refugees and asylum seekers

There are, by definition, no accurate figures for illegal trafficking. The combined figures for refugees and asylum seekers gives an indication of migration patterns

Throughout history people have been forced to flee from persecution. The three great monotheistic religions each have their own refugee stories.

- **Judaism**
  The book of *Exodus* tells of how the Hebrews escaped from slavery in Egypt in 1250 B.C.

- **Christianity**
  Joseph and Mary took the infant Jesus to safety in Egypt when Herod sent his soldiers to kill the newborn messiah.

- **Islam**
  The prophet Muhammad led his first converts to Islam out of Mecca to the city of Medina to escape persecution.

The Flight into Egypt by Tintoretto ➡

Refugees usually suffer poverty and frequently experience violent attacks. They are often victims of discrimination and generally feel isolated and lonely.

Many refugees wish to obtain *asylum*, i.e. to be given permission to live in another state, to have a right to obtain work there and to enjoy the same rights as any other citizen of their adopted country.

QUESTIONS

1. What is *prejudice*?
2. What is a *fair-minded* person?
3. What is *discrimination*?
4. Identify four groups who are often *victims* of discrimination.
5. What is a *refugee*?
6. Why do many refugees wish to obtain *asylum*?

Racism

We may define racism as

> *prejudice against people of another race or ethnic group.*

Racism has proven to be one of the most *destructive* forces in human history.

Racists believe that all human beings can be divided up into separate racial groups. Most of these groups will be considered *inferior*, while the group to which the racist belongs will be identified as *superior*, perhaps the *only* superior race.

Scientifically speaking, this is *nonsense*. Differences in skin colour, facial structure and so on are of no real significance. *All* people are members of the *same* biological species – *the human race.*

Hostility towards people of other races can range from a mild dislike to an extreme hatred, which can be expressed in acts of violence or in the passing of laws to deprive people of their rights. Where racism is put into practice in this way we have *racial discrimination.*

Historical examples of this would be:

■ The persecution of the Jewish people by the Nazis before and during World War Two.

■ The treatment of the native people of South Africa under the Apartheid regime in the twentieth century.

The Causes of Racism

A Family and Society

People are not born racists. They have to learn to be racists.

Many people unquestioningly accept racist attitudes from those around them as they are growing up.

B Stereotyped Thinking

A *stereotype* is a *general picture in the mind* that can affect a person's decisions on many matters.

If a person has a bad experience with someone from a particular race or ethnic group, then there may develop a strong tendency in that person to build up an image in his/her mind that *labels everyone* in that race or ethnic group as being the same.

As a result, the person ends up thinking badly from the *outset* of any future dealings he/she has with someone from that race or ethnic group.

Because of the tendency to form stereotypes, it is much easier for people to fall into prejudiced thinking than is often realised.

C Fear of difference

People generally grow up in communities where life follows a familiar pattern. But contact with people who have different languages, customs and religions can lead some people to become at first confused and then later resentful of those who depart from what they have been brought up to consider *normal*.

This often leads to unfounded, groundless *fear* of those who are different and this, in turn, can lead to unreasoning *hatred* that explodes into *violence*.

D Scapegoating

There is a tendency in many human beings to refuse to face up to their own feelings and to try to blame *others* for them. This is called *scapegoating*.

The worst example of scapegoating was Adolf Hitler's anti-Semitism (i.e. hatred of the Jewish people).

In the 1930s Hitler successfully persuaded the greater majority of Germans to lay the blame for all Germany's problems on the Jewish people. He found many willing helpers to conduct the campaign of racial discrimination that followed. In the end, he and his followers

murdered six million Jewish men, women and children in the concentration camps of central Europe.

Scapegoating appeals to people who do not want to face up to the reality of their own weaknesses. They find it very difficult to accept that they themselves can be narrow-minded, cruel and selfish. They cope with their own shortcomings by projecting them on to other people. This gives them a false sense of superiority. They may say to themselves

I don't have any problems. They're the ones with the problems. They're all lazy, stupid and violent.

People who think this way always need a target or *scapegoat* upon which to fix all their anger. Any group will do – overseas immigrants, disabled people or ethnic minorities for example. So long as they can feel good about themselves. However, this is only done by *running away* from the truth about themselves.

QUESTIONS

1. Explain the following:

    (a) *racism*, (b) *racial discrimination*.

2. Identify any *three* groups in society that suffer from discrimination.

3. In what way does *stereotyped thinking* contribute to racism in society?

4. Why does contact with people who have different languages, customs and religions sometimes lead to hatred and violence?

5. Explain the attraction to some people of making a *scapegoat* of people of a different race or ethnic group.

Opposing Racism

Racism has long been recognised as evil and destructive. In the *Old Testament*, the Jews were instructed to treat other races with respect:

*Do not ill-treat foreigners who are living in your land. Treat
them as you would a fellow-Israelite, and love them as you love
yourselves. Remember that you were once foreigners in the land
of Egypt. I am the Lord your God.*
Leviticus 19:33-34

In the *New Testament*, Jesus made it clear that the Kingdom of God is open to *all* people. Consider both

■ the healing of the Roman centurion's servant in *Luke* 7:1-10;

   and

■ the parable of the Good Samaritan in *Luke* 10:25-37.

Race or social status are of no importance to God. Every person is called to respect and offer help to those whom he/she meets. All are *equal* in God's sight.

Paul emphasised this point strongly in his letters to the early Christian communities.

*So there is no difference between Jews and Gentiles, between
slaves and free men, between men and women, you are all one in
union with Christ Jesus.*
Galatians 3:28

The Good Samaritan by Bassano
▼

*There is no longer any
distinction between Gentiles
and Jews, circumcised and
uncircumcised, barbarians,
savages, slaves and free men.*
Colossians 3:11

Each human being is created in God's *image and likeness*. All people are *children of God*; members of *one* human family and so are called to be brothers and sisters to one another.

It is for this reason that the Second Vatican Council stated:

*The Church reproves, as foreign to
the mind of Christ, any
discrimination against people or
any harassment of them on the
basis of their race, colour,
condition in life or religion.*

QUESTIONS

1. What did the author of *Leviticus* 19:33-34 want the Jews to remember when they encountered foreigners (i.e. non-Jews)?

2. Explain the point emphasised by Paul in *Galatians* 3:28 and *Colossians* 3:11.

3. Why should Christians and Jews oppose racism?

Profile: Combating Racism – Dr Martin Luther King

Martin Luther King was a great Christian leader, who inspired black Americans and gave them courage at a difficult time in their history.

There were twenty-two million black Americans by the mid-twentieth century, but they were without equal rights of citizenship with white Americans. Martin Luther King himself went to an all-Negro primary school in the city of Atlanta, where he had been born in 1929. He could remember seeing members of the Ku Klux Klan, a white supremacist organisation, attacking Negroes in the streets and was only six years old when he discovered that local white parents would not allow their children to play with him.

He became famous at the age of twenty-six. It happened because of a boycott of buses in Montgomery, Alabama, where he was pastor of a local Protestant church. Mrs Rosa Parks, a black seamstress in a large store, was returning home from work when a white passenger boarded the full bus. The law required a black person to give up a seat if the bus was full but Mrs Parks was tired, remained seated and politely refused to move. Police were called and she was arrested.

From that incident sprang the Montgomery bus boycott, which lasted for 382 days and changed the life of the black community. For over a year black people refused to use the buses. It was a costly sacrifice but they brought the bus company to the point of bankruptcy and, more importantly, the US Supreme Court intervened declaring segregation to be illegal. Notice that this change was brought about by *non-violent* means.

In the southern states, where segregation had been practised for so long, change could not be brought about overnight. The next dramatic move occurred in September 1957 at Little Rock in the state of Arkansas. Although schools had been officially desegregated, the governor of Arkansas used state troopers to bar nine Negro children from attending a white school. The US President sent federal troops to escort the children to school, and at last American citizens woke up to what was happening in their midst.

By now a Civil Rights' organisation had been formed called the Southern Christian Leadership Conference. It planned campaigns in one city after another, moving in to highlight

particular problems; for example sitting-in in 'Whites only' restaurants, travelling on 'Whites only' buses and crowding into 'Whites only' parks. In many places white Americans reacted violently but, such were the leadership qualities of Martin Luther King, that black people behaved with dignified restraint and refused to respond with violence. News pictures highlighted the contrast between the behaviour of blacks and whites to the detriment of the whites.

In the early 1960s John Kennedy was running for president. It was a close-run campaign and he needed the support of black voters. Martin Luther King seized the opportunity to win concessions for black people without having to resort to violence. He met the President in October 1962 and was able to press for action on Civil Rights' issues. The next year he was joined by many white people in a great march held in Washington D.C. to draw attention to a Civil Rights' Bill then being considered by Congress. At the Lincoln Memorial on this occasion he made one of his most famous speeches. 'I have a dream. It is a dream that is deeply rooted in the American dream. I have a dream that one day this nation will rise up, live out the true meaning of its creed: "We hold these truths to be self-evident, that all men are created equal".'

The Bill became law in 1964 but, by that time, President Kennedy had been assassinated and Martin Luther King fell foul of his successor through his opposition to the war in Vietnam. The Bill did not go as far as black people had hoped so the campaigning continued.

That year, at the age of thirty-five, Martin Luther King became the youngest person ever to be awarded the Nobel Peace Prize. The 54,000 dollars prize money went into Civil Rights' activities and the honour he received ensured maximum international publicity for the cause of equal rights of Negroes.

His next campaign was designed to give Negroes the vote. In Selma, Alabama, 15,000 black Americans were eligible to vote but, because of a variety of petty obstacles set out by white authorities, only 333 were allowed to do so. Martin Luther King led marches of Negroes to the courthouse in Selma, Alabama to ask for the vote. As more and more of them were arrested he wrote from prison 'There are more Negroes in jail with me than there are on the voting rolls'. From now on, whenever the Nobel Peace Prize winner was arrested or put in prison, it was news and provided adverse publicity for America throughout the world.

Nevertheless police and troops violently harassed marching protesters. Supporters, many of them white, streamed in from other parts of America and King's non-violent upholding of the rights and human dignity of black people became an embarrassment to the state government in Alabama. At last the US President announced that he would give top priority to a Voting Rights' Bill.

At the time of his assassination in 1968, Martin Luther King had learned to live with threats not only to his own life but also to the lives of his family. Like Gandhi whose example of non-violence he followed, he was killed by a gunman. However, as with Mahatma Gandhi, the success of his cause was assured. Not all the problems of race relations in America have been solved but the attitudes of many white people have been changed. It is no longer acceptable in the United States to behave in a racist fashion.

Adapted from Diana Morgan, *Christian Perspectives on Contemporary Issues*

QUESTIONS

1. When and where was Martin Luther King born?

2. What is the Ku Klux Klan?

3. Why did Martin Luther King become famous at the age of twenty-six?

4. Explain how the black Civil Rights' movement used non-violent means to achieve their goal of equal rights.

5. What award did Martin Luther King win at the age of thirty-five?

6. In what year was Martin Luther King assassinated?

7. What did Martin Luther King achieve?

CHAPTER FIFTEEN

THE RIGHTS
OF WOMEN

Introduction

Consider the following quotations taken from the writings of influential men:

- *The female is a female by virtue of a certain lack of qualities.*
  Aristotle

- *A man neither consults women about, nor trusts them with, serious matters.*
  The Earl of Chesterfield

These statements are examples of *sexism*. Sexism can be defined as

> *the view that one sex is inferior to the other, in particular, that women are less able in most ways than men.*

Feminism

The term *sexism* was first used in the 1960s by *feminists*, i.e. those who work to obtain equal rights and fair treatment for women.

Feminists point out that, until very recently, Western society was largely

patriarchal, i.e. dominated by men, who made all the important decisions without consulting women.

For thousands of years, women were regarded chiefly as possessions, as the personal property of their fathers or husbands. Women were denied the right to choose how to live their lives. A woman could be married off without any consideration for her happiness. Unfortunately, this is still the case in many parts of the world.

Feminists point out that sexist attitudes towards women can still be seen in the way some people use language. For example, to use the word *mankind* when referring to the *whole* human race, men *and women*.

Also, many men still assume that certain jobs should *only* be performed by men. They can sometimes place serious obstacles in the way of women, which men would not encounter. It remains difficult for women to achieve positions of influence in society as a result.

However, thanks to many decades of tireless campaigning, feminists have achieved notable reforms. In the developed world, it is now recognised by law that:

- Women over eighteen years of age are entitled to vote.
- Women can stand for election to the national parliament.
- Women are entitled to equal pay for work of equal value.
- Women have equal employment opportunities and cannot be discriminated against on the basis of gender.

Elsewhere, however, many of these basic rights have yet to be achieved.

The Global Situation

Women form half of the earth's population, and yet:

- Two out of every three illiterate people are women, because of their lack of educational opportunities.
- Women do two-thirds of the world's working-hours, yet they only receive one-tenth of the income and they own a mere one-hundredth of its property.

Womanhood: a perilous path
▼

■ While women everywhere are overburdened in the home, in poor countries they are also the main food producers. But most of the technology, finance and training in agriculture is given to men.

■ In Third World primary schools there are only five girls for every seven boys. So lack of education and heavy responsibilities keep women isolated and weak – unable to get together to take their rightful share.

■ Violation of the human rights of women and female children are extensive and severe. Many women are targeted because they are leaders in the struggle for freedom and justice. Others are victimised because they are seen to be vulnerable, because they can be used to put pressure on male relatives, or because of the inferior status of women in their societies. Some are imprisoned, tortured and killed simply because they were unfortunate enough to be in the wrong place at the wrong time.

■ The Catholic Church has condemned the killing of unborn female babies following gender testing. Some couples choose to abort a female baby because they have a preference for a male child.

QUESTIONS

1. What is *sexism*?
2. What does it mean to say that, until very recently, Western society was *patriarchal*?
3. What is a *feminist*?
4. Identify *four* important rights which women are guaranteed by law in Western society.

JOURNAL WORK

The eighteenth-century feminist thinker Mary Wollstonecraft stated:

I do not wish women to have power over men; but over themselves.

What does women having *power over themselves* mean? In your answer, consider how women across the globe are deprived of their most basic rights.

Women in Islam

Read the following extract.

A Muslim woman in traditional dress

A Muslim wife retains ownership of any money or property that she acquired before marriage. But it is the husband who is responsible for the economic security of the family.

Although the Qur'an exhorts marriage partners to treat each other with kindness and equity, love and compassion, it also recognises that some marriages do not work. Therefore, Islamic law sets down procedures for divorce. It is easier for men to divorce their wives, but wives may initiate divorces too.

Although in modern, Western eyes Muslim women seem oppressed, the Qur'an actually protects women better than previous practices. For instance, unwanted female babies were frequently buried alive by the Bedouin. Islam also opposed unlimited polygamy (i.e marriage of a man to more than one woman) as practised by Arabs in Muhammad's time. Muhammad said 'Of other women who seem good in your eyes, marry but two, or three, or four; and if ye still fear that ye shall not act equitably, then only one.' (Qur'an 4:3)

The dress restrictions for Muslim women reflect the attitude that women should not provide temptation for men. Thus, outside the home, women are supposed to be covered in loose-fitting garments from head to foot. Today, most Islamic countries allow women's hands and faces to be exposed, although veiled women are still a common sight. In Islam, women should appear beautiful only to their husbands.

Loretta Pastva, *Great Religions of the World*

QUESTIONS

1. What does the *Qur'an* teach about marriage and divorce?
2. Why is it said that *the Qur'an actually protects women better than previous practices*?
3. What did Muhammad teach about marriage?

4. What are the dress restrictions on Muslim women?

5. Why do Muslims believe such dress restrictions should exist for women?

Women in Christianity

Jesus lived in a patriarchal society in which men had the dominant role. Women were generally regarded by men as useful possessions and largely treated as second-class citizens. We can see this reflected in the *Old Testament*. For example:

- The law regarding rape which said that an unmarried woman was her father's property.
  Deuteronomy 22:28-29

- The law which stated that a man could divorce his wife if he wished, but did not say that a wife was equally entitled to divorce her husband.
  Deuteronomy 24:1

Some early Christian writers were very much influenced by this attitude to women.

For example, Clement of Alexandria wrote:

> *Every woman should be overwhelmed with shame at the thought that she is a woman.*

Some Christian commentators tried to use *Genesis* 3:1-24 to show that it was the first woman (*Eve*) who was responsible for bringing sin into the world.

> *It was not Adam who was led astray but the woman (Eve) who was led astray and fell into sin.*
> *1 Timothy* 2:14

The story of *the Fall* was wrongly interpreted to support the idea that women were weaker than men.

Feminist writers have argued that this kind of thinking has played a major role in encouraging sexism and contributed significantly to the unfair treatment of women in the past.

Today, however, *no* reputable Christian scholar would lend any credibility whatsoever to an interpretation of *Genesis* chapter three that seeks to undermine the dignity of women.

On the contrary, the American Catholic bishops have declared:

> *It is a profound sin to label women as the source of evil in the world, as intellectually inferior, psychologically unstable and inclined to sensuality.*

They stated that sexism is a profound sin because it violates the basic teachings of the Christian faith. They also apologised for past wrongs.

> *We regret and confess our individual and collective failures to respond to women, as they deserve.*

The criticisms of feminists have caused the Christian churches to rethink their attitudes towards the rights of women.

The Canadian Catholic bishops have declared:

> *The state of submission and oppression to which women are subjected in the world constitutes a sinful situation, something to correct. The Church must, in fidelity to the word of God, recognise the modern feminist movement as a positive reality. We are dealing on the whole, with an advance in civilisation; and it's a forward step in the establishment of the Kingdom of God.*

In recent years, Christian scripture scholars have been paying greater attention than before to what the *Gospels* have to say about how Jesus related to women. They have discovered that Christianity has a far more radical message about the relationship between men and women than was previously either realised or recognised.

QUESTIONS

1. How were women generally regarded in *Old Testament* times? Give one example to illustrate your answer.

2. (a) How did some Christian commentators once interpret *Genesis* 3:1-24?

   (b) Does the Catholic Church today accept this interpretation of *Genesis* 3:1-24?

3. Why does the Catholic Church today teach that sexism is *a profound sin*?

Jesus and Women in the Gospels

The evangelists portray Jesus as being very different to his contemporaries in his attitude to women. He did *not* share the view that women were second-class citizens which was so common among men of that era. Jesus treated women as people in their own right, as *equals*.

Consider the following:

- Jesus included women among his disciples (see *Luke* 8:1-3).

- Jesus defied the social conventions of the day by having private conversations with women, where he listened to them, took what they said seriously and treated them with respect (see *John* 4:5-42).

- Jesus enjoyed the company of women and made no distinctions between his male and female followers (see *Luke* 10:38-42).

- Jesus accepted and readily acknowledged help from women (see *Luke* 7:36-50).

- Jesus emphasised equality of respect for women. When he said that a man could commit adultery against his wife, he was saying something *new*. The Jewish rabbis of that time only recognised adultery as being a sin committed by *a wife against her husband*.

- Jesus took a firm stand against the unjust treatment of women. For example, the Adulterous Woman (*John* 8:1-11) and the Healing of the Crippled Woman on the Sabbath (*Luke* 13:10-17).

It should also be remembered that:

- Jesus' female disciples were the ones who loyally stood at the foot of the cross when his male disciples had fled into hiding.

- It was some of Jesus' female disciples who were the first witnesses to his resurrection and the first to believe that he had risen.

Jesus came into the world to set free the oppressed and to raise up the humble. This was beautifully expressed in *the Magnificat*, spoken by Jesus' mother, Mary (*Luke* 1:46-55).

▲ *Crucifixion with Mary Magdalene* by Signorelli

Jesus wanted to show us that the Kingdom of God broke down all the barriers that separated people, whether they are race, poverty or *gender*.

Jesus made it clear that *both* men and women are made *in the image and likeness of God* (Genesis 1:27).

The equality of the sexes is basic Christian teaching. As Paul wrote:

> *You were baptised into union with Christ, and now you are clothed, so to speak, with the life of Christ himself. So there is no difference between Jews and Gentiles, between slaves and free men, between men and women; you are all one in union with Christ Jesus.*
> *Galatians 3:27-28*

QUESTIONS

1. What is the key idea expressed in the *Magnificat* (*Luke* 1:46-55)?

2. State any *three* examples taken from the Gospels which demonstrate how Jesus treated men and women as *equals*.

3. What is the central point made by Paul in *Galatians* 3:27-28?

The Ordination of Women

The Catholic Church and the Orthodox Churches have stated that they will not ordain women. Both continue the traditional practice of accepting only men as candidates for the priesthood.

Among the mainstream Protestant Churches, Anglicans, Methodists and Baptists have women ministers.

CHAPTER SIXTEEN

THE RIGHTS
OF THE ELDERLY

Introduction

Modern society tends to emphasise strength, speed, physical appearance and spending power. Most of these qualities have declined by the time people have reached old age. This should in no way lessen the respect due to the elderly, but all too often it *does*.

Some commentators are concerned that our society is tending, increasingly, to push aside its *senior citizens* (i.e. those aged sixty-five years and over). Many of them live alone, while many more reside in homes for the elderly. All too often they are forgotten by their relatives. Some people treat them with contempt, considering old people to be nuisances with nothing to contribute. This prejudice against our senior citizens is called *ageism*.

What Do You See?

Read the following poem. It was written by an elderly woman named Kate. She spent her last two years in a hospital ward. She couldn't speak but, on occasions, she was noticed writing on a notepad. After she died, this poem was discovered in her bedside locker.

What do you see nurses, what do you see?
What are you thinking, when you're looking as me:
A crabbit old woman, not very wise,
Uncertain of habit, with far-away eyes,
Who dribbles her food and makes no reply
When you say in a loud voice, 'I do wish you'd try'.
Who seems not to notice the things that you do
And forever is losing a stocking or shoe.
Who, unresisting or not, lets you do as you will,
With bathing and feeding the long day to fill.
Is that what you're thinking, is that what you see?
Then open you eyes, nurse, you're not looking at me.
I'll tell you who I am as I sit here so still,
As I use at your bidding, as I eat at your will.
I'm a small child of ten with a father and mother,
Brothers and sisters who love one another.
A young girl of sixteen with wings at her feet,
Dreaming that soon now a lover she'll meet.
A bride soon at twenty, my heart gives a leap,
Remembering the vows that I'd promised to keep.
At twenty-five now, I have young of my own,
Who need me to build a secure, happy home.
A young woman of thirty, my young now grow fast,
Bound to each other with ties that should last.
At forty my young ones now grown, will soon be gone,
But my man stays beside me to see I don't mourn.
At fifty once more babies play round my knee,
Again we know children, my loved one and me.
Dark days are upon me, my husband is dead,
I look at the future, I shudder with dread.
For my young are all busy rearing young of their own,
I think of the years and the love I have known.
I'm an old woman now, but nature is cruel,
'Tis her jest to make old age look like a fool.
The body it crumbles, grace and vigour depart,
There now is a stone, where I once had a heart,
But inside this old carcass, a young girl still dwells,
And now and again my battered heart swells.
I remember the joys, I remember the pain,
And I'm loving and living life over again.
I think of the years, all too few – gone too fast,
And accept the stark fact that nothing can last.
So open you eyes nurse, open and see,
Not a crabbit old woman, look closer – see ME.

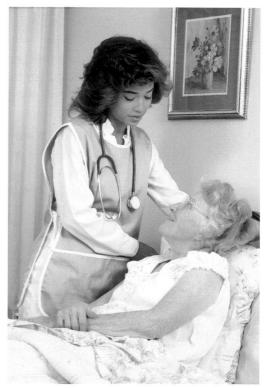

QUESTIONS

1. In some less economically developed societies, the elderly are respected for their wisdom and experience. Why does this no longer seem to be the case in much of Western society?

2. What is *ageism*?

3. What did Kate believe the nurses thought about her? Do you think they saw her as a person like them? Give reasons for your answer.

4. (a) What were the events in Kate's later life that caused those years to be *dark days*?

   (b) What kind of help should she have received during that time?

Problems experienced by the elderly

1. **Physical ageing:** There are no diseases that affect only people above a certain age, but there are some conditions that become increasingly common with advancing age. Arthritis is common and about half the strokes that occur happen in people over seventy-five years of age. Other ailments that occur include deafness, difficulty in understanding speech, poor memory and reduced mobility. The end result may often be complete dependence on other people. However, many elderly people are not so affected that they could not remain living in their own homes if there were adequate domestic support services available to help them cope.

2. **Hypothermia:** In the elderly, the part of the brain that controls body temperature is often less efficient than in younger people. In cold weather, body temperature can fall to dangerously low levels, and hypothermia is responsible for several premature deaths of elderly people each winter.

3. **Inadequate diet:** Old people are often malnourished, whether due to poor co-ordination, digestive problems, shopping difficulties or lack of money.

4. **Reduced income:** If, as is often the case, no provision has been made for retirement or old age, the elderly must survive on the old age pension. Their standard of living may well, therefore, become lower than that to which they have been accustomed.

5. **Fear:** Old people who live alone are vulnerable to attack, as they are not able to defend themselves. Some, especially in inner city or isolated areas, live in fear of being robbed and assaulted.

6. **Inadequate housing:** Accommodation for the elderly may be sub-standard, without even a private bathroom or kitchen, heating or telephone. It may be damp and in need of repair, and too often is located away from where the elderly person has lived all his/her life.

7. **Loneliness and social isolation:** While some old people remain alone by choice, others are forced to live alone because their families have emigrated, their spouse has died or they are unable to leave their homes for some reason. Loneliness may lead to depression and apathy.

   Where elderly people have been forced to move into a home, they can become isolated from both their families and from society as a whole, and their loss of privacy and sense of self-worth can similarly lead to depression and loss of interest in living.

   Read the following extract.

   Mother Teresa is credited with saying the great disease of our time is loneliness. She once told the following story:

'One day I visited a house where our sisters shelter the aged. This is one of the nicest houses in England, filled with beautiful and precious things. Yet there was not one smile on the faces of the elderly people. All of them were looking towards the door.

I asked the sister in charge "Why are they like that?" She answered: "They are always waiting for someone to come and visit them. Loneliness eats them up and day after day they do not stop looking. Nobody comes. Abandonment is an awful poverty".'

COMMENT

Old age is seen by many as a problem rather than a natural process in life, which must be faced. One of the true tests of any society that claims to be *caring* is to examine how it treats its elderly people, particularly those who are no longer able to defend their own rights.

QUESTIONS

1. The fourth commandment calls on people to *Honour your father and your mother*. How does this translate into *practical* care for the elderly?
2. In what way would *sheltered accommodation*, which provides separate housing, but has support services and contact with other people, show respect for the dignity of elderly people?

JOURNAL WORK

The strain of caring for someone who needs help with feeding, washing and going to the toilet, who may sleep badly and need attention during the night as well as in the daytime can bring even a loving relative to the point of violence.

F. van Zwanenberg, *Caring for the Aged*

What kind of support services should be made available to help those caring for an elderly relative?

Profile: Willie Bermingham, Founder of ALONE

The following article was published on the day after his death.

William Patrick (Willie) Bermingham, the founder of ALONE, the organisation for helping the poor and elderly, has died. He was forty-eight.
   While his official job was that of fireman at Dublin's Tara Street fire station, *most of Mr Bermingham's life revolved around helping isolated old people who were suffering from loneliness and fear*. The stories of his courage and

generosity are legion. Friends say the stories that remain untold are even more numerous and dramatic.

ALONE stands for '*A Little Offering Never Ends*'. The organisation has provided housing, clothing, food and general comfort for hundreds of elderly Dubliners over the last dozen years.

Even on his death-bed, and knowing he hadn't long to live, his spirit was undiminished. He was still thinking of the plight of the poor and elderly in the city. Some weeks ago, responding to media queries about his health, he said, 'I am quite ill, but it will be of short duration. I would like everyone to know that the work of ALONE will proceed, immaterial of whether I live or die. I appeal to the public to look after the vulnerable old as the most appropriate way of showing their sympathy to me.'

His unselfish, dedicated work was recognised during his lifetime. He was awarded the *People of the Year Award* in 1979; later he received the

International Fireman of the Year Award, and an *Honorary Doctorate of Law* was conferred on him by Trinity College, Dublin, in the city's Millennium Year, 1988 (see photo).

ALONE's twenty-two-unit complex for old people, soon to be built at Kilmainham Lane, will be named in his memory.

Born in Inchicore in 1942, he was the third eldest of seven children. His father was a bellman, selling coal, logs, timber and scrap. Mr Bermingham followed in his father's footsteps, but soon packed in the business because there was 'no future in it'. He didn't always see eye to eye with his father because he kept giving away coal and logs to people for whom he felt sorry, especially the old.

ALONE was founded in 1977. In May of that year, Mr Bermingham was working with the brigade's ambulance service. *He was called to retrieve the bodies of several old people who died unnoticed in appalling poverty and isolation.*

He came upon eight cases in three months of old people who had died in dire conditions.

A great anger hit him and this remained with him all his life. He set up his one-man organisation ALONE, in an effort to help the numerous elderly people in need of urgent attention. He plastered posters all over the city, pointing out the seriousness of the problem. Donations flooded in. People rang him telling him of old people in distress. He always made it his business to get there without delay.

He maintained that time was the essence and detested red tape. 'ALONE's biggest problem', he once told the *Irish Times*, 'is in getting State health and welfare agencies to recognise the fantasy that their present systems are adequate to rescue neglected old people from conditions unfit for animals.'

He vigorously lobbied the Eastern Health Board, Dublin Corporation, the Lord Mayor's office, the Taoiseach and TDs. He had contact with just about everyone in authority at one time or another, *urging them – demanding – that they take immediate action on some specific problem*. Much of his lobbying was not exactly cordial or amicable. Mr Bermingham was many things, but *he could never have been accused of being a diplomat*. When he wanted something done, he wanted it done NOW. He *begged, cajoled, tormented and made bureaucrats feel uneasy*. He usually got what he wanted.

He was the virtual Robin Hood of Dublin. He was regarded by those in authority as a cross between a saint and a bloody nuisance. There was also a feeling among some people in the various Dublin authorities that Mr Bermingham was taking credit for much of what they were doing. This was an accusation he did not let worry him; it never deterred him from making his case, week in, week out.

He had always been a man of action. He stepped on a lot of important toes in his time, but he felt this was inevitable if he was to get what he wanted – quickly. In his latter years, *he calmed down a little and his rage was not as intense*, but right up to his death he was getting things done.

His family suffered from his dedication to the old and lonely. Between working for the fire brigade and looking after the affairs of ALONE, his family did not see a lot of him. Although, again, in the latter years he tried to rectify that to some extent. However, he had their full support and his wife, and family did a lot of effective work for the elderly behind the scenes.

Adapted from the *Irish Times*, 24 April 1990

QUESTIONS

1. Explain the meaning of ALONE.
2. What experience inspired Willie Bermingham to found ALONE?
3. How did Willie Bermingham draw attention to the plight of the elderly?
4. How did some people in authority react to his work?
5. In an interview shortly before his death, Willie Bermingham said that his original aim in setting up ALONE was that it would *'go out of business'* when it would no longer be needed. *'But I can't see that day coming,'* he added. Why do you think he said this?
6. Why did Willie Bermingham persist in working for better care for the elderly?

JOURNAL WORK

What kind of quality of life do you hope for in your old age?

CHAPTER SEVENTEEN

STEWARDS OF CREATION

Introduction

Passing Storm in
Yosemite by Bierstadt
➡

Christians believe that the *environment* (i.e. the world and everything in it) did not happen by chance. It was *created* by God.

> *In the beginning God created the heavens and the earth ... and*
> *God saw that it was good.*
> *Genesis 1:1-10*

The environment is a gift from God. It is *sacred*, i.e. worthy of honour and respect. Yet, consider the state of the environment today.

> *All the living systems on land and in the seas are being ruthlessly*
> *exploited. The damage is extensive and often cannot be undone. The*

attack on the natural world is whittling away at the very base of our living world and endangering its fruitfulness for future generations .... Faced with these challenges where the very future of life is at stake, we call on all to take a stand on the side of life.

The Catholic Bishops of the Philippines

Environmental Problems

In order to survive, human beings need air, water, food, shelter and medicines. The Earth can provide all these needs, but its natural resources are not unlimited. Some are in danger of running out, while others have been so badly abused that they have disappeared altogether.

Some of the areas of greatest concern are:

■ The Destruction of the Rainforests

The world's rainforests are being cut down at such a rate that, within fifty years, they will have disappeared entirely. This would be a catastrophe. The rainforests provide oxygen that enables us to breathe.

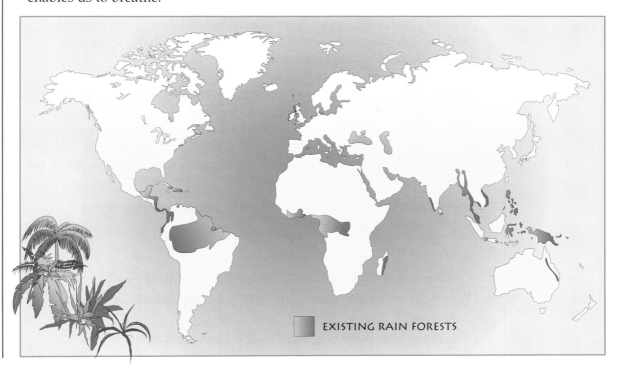

EXISTING RAIN FORESTS

Unfortunately, most of the countries in which the rainforests are located show little willingness to stop this policy. They owe heavy debts to Western banks and say that they need the money from deforestation programmes to pay off their loans.

■ The Danger of Nuclear Waste

The nuclear power industry produces large quantities of radioactive waste. Most of this is stored in special facilities.

This waste has to be transported to such sites. It will remain highly radioactive and lethal for thousands of years. Future generations will have to cope with the consequences of today's decisions.

■ The Harm Caused by Acid Rain

Industrialised nations burn large quantities of fossil fuels (e.g. oil and coal). These produce *sulphur oxides* that fall as acid rain, killing trees and poisoning waterways.

■ The Prevention of Future Medical Breakthroughs

Half of all medicines come from plants, e.g. *morphine* comes from poppies and *quinine* comes from trees grown in the Amazonian rainforest. The on-going destruction of the rainforests may deprive the human race of cures for serious illnesses in the future.

■ The Damage to the Economy

Many jobs today are dependent on a clean, high quality environment. These include dairying, meat processing, tourism, pharmaceuticals, electronics, aquaculture and forestry.

The growing awareness of these problems has encouraged the development of the *Green or Environmental Movement*, which campaigns to protect the planet.

Environmental campaigners have made it clear that, if the human race is to have a future, major changes will have to take place. The most important will be the general adoption of a whole new outlook as to how people relate to the fragile environment of this planet.

QUESTIONS

1. What is the *environment*?
2. Why do Christians consider the environment to be *sacred*?
3. Identify three important sources of pollution in modern industrial nations.
4. What are the economic benefits of a clean environment?

Fighting the pollution

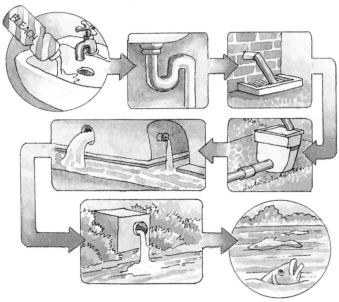

Targets in the drive against lethal filth

Power stations
Tight controls have been introduced on discharges of water which were taken from rivers for cooling and returned several degrees warmer, driving out oxygen.

Heavy industry
Emissions from factories clustered around estuaries have been more rigorously controlled.

Sewage systems
Millions have been spent on updating pipes that allow untreated waste to pour into waterways.

Farms
Teams of inspectors have visited farms to prevent pesticides, slurry and silage from entering rivers and creating havoc.

The Delicate Balance

There was a rule for people who were climbing the mountain that above a certain point no living things were to be killed. The climbers had to carry all their food.

One day someone who was walking on the mountain above that point was caught in a violent snowstorm. For three days he lived in a makeshift shelter with no food in near freezing conditions. On the third

day the blizzard ended. He saw a very old rat crawling out of a hole and thought there would be no harm in killing the rat so that he could feed himself and get down the mountain. Somehow he managed to get a stone and kill the rat. He made it down the mountain and did not think any more about it.

Some time later he was called before the tribunal of guides, that is, of people responsible for the mountain and the path. He was called to account for the killing of the rat, an event that by this time he had forgotten. It seemed there had been serious consequences. The rat, being very old, was not strong enough to catch the healthy insects, and so it fed on the diseased insect population. When the rat was killed there was no natural check on the diseased insects. Disease spread throughout the whole species and they all died off.

The insects had been responsible for pollinating and fertilising much of the plant growth on the mountainside. When the insects died off, without fertilisation, the vegetation started to diminish. The plant life had been holding the soil in place and when the vegetation began to die the soil started to erode.

Eventually, there was a great landslide, which killed many people who were climbing up the mountain, and blocked the path for a long time. All of this the outcome of the seemingly insignificant act of killing the old rat.

Rene Daumal, *Mount Analogue*

More and more people are beginning to realise that the human race can no longer afford to wreak havoc on the delicate balance of life on Earth.

All living things – humans, animals and plants – are part of a vast, complex chain where all living things *depend* upon one another.

The loss of one species of animal or plant can have a devastating effect upon the other living things that depend upon it. If enough links in the chain of life are broken, then the very survival of the human race will be at stake.

QUESTIONS

1. What is meant by the delicate balance of nature?

2. Read the following extract and answer the question below.

   All things are connected like the blood which unites one family. All things are connected. Whatever befalls the earth befalls the sons of the earth. Man did not weave the web of life; he is merely a strand in it. Whatever he does to the web he does to himself.

   (Chief Seattle, of the Duwamish tribe when the US Government was forcing him to accept the purchase of his tribe's lands in 1854.)

   What point does Chief Seattle make about the importance of preserving the delicate balance of nature?

Stewardship

A *change* in the way most people relate to the natural world is needed. Christians believe that the basis for this *new relationship* between humans and the two million other species that share our planet, can be found in the Bible.

In the *Old Testament* it is written of the first humans that:

God blessed them, and God said to them; Be Fruitful and multiply and fill the earth and subdue it; and have dominion over

> *the fish of the sea and over the birds of the air and over every*
> *living thing that moves upon the earth.*
> Genesis 1:28

However, God makes it clear that:

> *the land belongs to me and you are only strangers and guests.*
> Leviticus 25:23

Then, in the *New Testament*, there are three important passages to consider:

- *Luke* 12:36-44
- *Luke* 16:1-8
- *1 Corinthians* 4:1-5

Sacred scripture makes it very clear that human beings are *not* the owners of the world. Rather, they are called to be *God's stewards*.

The word *steward* means someone who

- has been appointed to care for the world on God's behalf;
- should not give in to purely selfish interests but be wise and trustworthy;
- has a responsibility to hand on the world in a living and fertile state to future generations.

Bernhard Anderson has written:

> *This call to stewardship is a privilege bestowed on humankind by God.*
> *As with all privileges, human beings will be held accountable for their*
> *stewardship. If they are caring and cultivate harmony in all their*
> *dealings with each other and the Earth, then they grow in the image*
> *and likeness of God.*
>
>   *Cry of the Environment*

Profile: Chico Mendes, Steward of the Rainforest

Francisco 'Chico' Mendes was born on the 15 December 1944 on a rubber estate in Xapuri, Acre in north-west Brazil. His parents had come from the dry north-east of Brazil, sent to cut rubber for the allied war effort. Chico was born and brought up in the rainforest learning the skills of a 'seringueiro', a rubber tapper.

> *My life began just like that of all rubber tappers, as a virtual slave*
> *bound to the bidding of my master. I started work at nine years old,*

and like my father before me, instead of learning my ABC I learned how to extract latex from a rubber tree. From the last century until 1970, schools were forbidden on any rubber estate in the Amazon. The rubber estate owners wouldn't allow it. First, because if a rubber tapper's children went to school, they would learn to read, write and add up and would discover to what extent they were being exploited. This wasn't in the bosses' interests. Also, it was better for production to have the children available for work rather than going to school.

Chico loved the rainforest but hated the way the rubber tappers were being treated. He wanted to do something about it but wasn't sure what. During the 1960s and 1970s things began to change in Xapuri and Chico found a way to stand up for the rights of the rubber tappers. He also found a new cause. Cattle ranchers from southern Brazil, encouraged by government grants began to buy up the rubber estates. This had disastrous effects on the rainforest and the people who lived in it and who depended on it for their livelihood. The trees were cleared in order to create grazing land for the cattle.

Rubber tappers were evicted, often brutally. Others retreated further into the forest and continued producing on their own account, victims of exploitation by local merchants. In the early 1970s Xapuri Rural Workers' Union was founded and Chico was soon elected its president. A modest and unpretentious man, he was nevertheless a natural leader. As the conflicts over land intensified, the union developed the technique of the *empate*, sometimes translated as 'stalemate' or 'standoff'. Chico describes it like this.

> *When a community is threatened by deforestation it gets in touch*
> *with other communities in the area. They all get together in a mass*
> *meeting in the middle of the forest and organise teams of people to*
> *take the lead in confronting the workers cutting down the trees — all*
> *this in a peaceful but organised way. These teams try and convince*
> *the workers employed by the landowners to leave the area. The rubber*
> *tappers also dismantle the camps used by those workers to force them*
> *out. We are often attacked by the police because the landowners*
> *always apply to the courts for police protection. The judicial system*
> *has always done what the landowners wanted and sent in the police*
> *and there have been a lot of arrests.*
>
> *One important point is that the whole community – men, women*
> *and children – takes part in the empate. The women stay at the front*
> *to prevent the police from shooting us. The police know if they open*
> *fire, they will kill women and children.*
>
> *I remember on a least four occasions, we were arrested and forced*
> *to lie on the ground with them beating us. They threw our bodies,*
> *covered in blood, into a lorry but we all sang hymns. We got to the*
> *police station, perhaps more than a hundred people, but they didn't*
> *have enough room to keep us there and we had to stand up in the*
> *corridors. In the end they had to let us go free.*

Under his leadership the union prevented the destruction of 12,000 square
kilometres of rainforest. Schools and health clinics were set up for the
rubber tappers and their children. Co-operatives were organised to ensure
that workers get fair prices for their produce. Also meetings began with the
chiefs of the native people of the rainforest. Indians and rubber tappers
had been enemies for over a century.

> *In Acre the leaders of the rubber tappers and Indian peoples met and*
> *concluded that neither was to blame for this. The real culprits were*
> *the rubber estate owners, the bankers and all the other powerful*
> *interest groups that had exploited us both. People understood this*
> *very quickly, and from the beginning of 1986 the alliance of the*
> *peoples of the forest got stronger and stronger.*

The other major development of the union was the idea of an 'extractive
reserve'.

> *We accept that the Amazon could not be turned into some kind of*
> *sanctuary that nobody could touch. On the other hand, we knew it was*
> *important to stop the deforestation that is threatening the Amazon and*

all human life on the planet. We realised that in order to guarantee the future of the Amazon we had to find a way to preserve the forests, while at the same time producing a plan to develop the economy. So we came up with the idea of extractive reserves. These are forests lands, which would be set aside and put under public ownership. Rubber tappers, Indians and people who harvest Brazil nuts, jute and other products would have the right to 'extract a living' there.

Chico and his union had to wait until 1988 before their idea became a reality. After a series of shootings and killings and after one particularly difficult *empate* at a rubber estate called Cachocira, the government finally decided to set aside three extractive reserves, one of them at Cachocira. The victory for the rubber tappers was also the death sentence for Chico as the family of the estate's owner sought to avenge their defeat. At 5.45 p.m. on Thursday 22 December 1988 Chico got up from his evening meal and went to the door of his house. Two men appeared at the doorway. Shots were fired. Chico died in the arms of his wife and a friend in front of his two young children.

He knew he had been marked for death. In a letter to a friend shortly before his death he wrote

My dream is to see this entire forest conserved because we know it can guarantee the future of all the people who live in it. Not only that, I believe that in a few years the Amazon can become an economically viable region not only for us, but for the nation, for all of humanity, and for the whole planet ... I don't want flowers at my funeral because I know they would be taken from the forest ... I want to live.

All quotations from *Fight for the Forest – Chico Mendes in his own words.*
Adapted from *A New Earth*, The Gateway Series 2

QUESTIONS

1. Why did the estate owners not want the children of workers to be educated?
2. What is *empate*?
3. How did *empate* work?
4. What was achieved under Chico Mendes' leadership?
5. Explain the idea of *extractive reserve*.
6. Why was Chico Mendes murdered?

Caring for Animals

Human beings have rights. In recent years, there has been considerable debate as to whether or not animals also have rights and, if so, the precise nature and extent of their rights. The debate on animal rights centres on six areas:

(i) The breeding and killing of animals for food.

(ii) The use of animals in medical research.

(iii) The testing of cosmetics, detergents and non-medical household goods on animals.

(iv) The breeding and killing of animals for fur.

(v) The hunting and killing of animals for sport.

(vi) The breeding and training of animals for entertainment.

Medical research conducted on animals *has* contributed to several important breakthroughs in the treatment of human illnesses.

■ Experiments conducted on *dogs* were responsible for advances in kidney transplants and open-heart surgery.

■ Research on *monkeys* led to a vaccine against rubella and the development of life-support machines for prematurely born babies.

■ Experiments on *rabbits* played an important role in the development of chemotherapy for leukaemia sufferers.

Currently, animals are being used in research into AIDS, cancer and heart disease.

However, to achieve such breakthroughs, animals are subjected to laboratory experiments in which they are injected with drugs, exposed to radiation or toxic chemicals and infected with diseases.

For example, rabbits have been used for testing the effects of shampoo ingredients, by dropping chemicals into their eyes.

Those in favour of experimentation on animals point out that animals are different from human beings.

For example:

■ Animals act only on instinct.

■ Animals do not have a capacity for sophisticated language.

■ Animals cannot make plans or take responsibility for their actions.

■ Animals are incapable of showing love in the way human beings can.

As a result, many people conclude that animals do not deserve the same respect as human beings.

There is ample evidence, however, that animals *can* feel pain, fear and pleasure.

Christians do not deny the real differences between humans and animals. However, while the *Bible* teaches that humans are at the pinnacle (i.e. the highest point) of creation, it does *not* mean that people can do whatever they please with

animals. In *Genesis* 2:15 God commands people to *care* for all the creatures in the world. The animals are *not* to be callously exploited. Each creature has a role to play in the complex web of life.

> *Lord, may we love all your creation, all the earth and every grain of sand in it. May we love every leaf, every ray of your light. May we love the animals; you have given them the rudiments of thought and joy untroubled. Let us not trouble them; let us not harass them; let us not deprive them of their happiness; let us not work against your intent. For we acknowledge unto you that all is like an ocean, all is flowing and blending, and that to withhold any measure of love from anything in your universe is to withhold that same measure from you.*
>
> Fyodor Dostoevsky, Russian author

The Bible stories express the belief that God has given human beings authority over creation, not to abuse it but to care for it as *stewards*. Caring involves respect for life and the loss of that sense of respect leads to the *brutalising* of human beings.

People must show a greater sensitivity to the other living things on Earth.

Take care of all that has been entrusted to you.
1 Timothy 6:20

QUESTIONS

1. Identify three ways in which animals are different from humans.
2. Examine each of the six areas of concern regarding animal rights listed above. Which of them, do you think, are justified? Explain you choices.
3. Many people are comparatively untroubled by the use of mice in experiments. An estimated twenty-five million mice are put to death in tests each year. But they become very angry if rabbits, cats or dogs are used. Why does this happen? Is there really any difference?
4. According to *Genesis* 2:15 how should people treat animals?

JOURNAL WORK

If someone you love was in danger of dying if doctors did not use a drug tested on animals, what would you want them to do? Explain your answer.

Don't Waste Waste – Recycle

'Everything must go somewhere' – nothing actually disappears when it is thrown away. In fact this contributes to many of our present environmental problems. Today in our Western 'First World' society we consume, burn, wear out, replace and discard things at a rate unprecedented in our history. The time we are living in has been referred to as the 'Waste Age'. Our consumption is keeping pace with production! Advertisers, as a mouthpiece of the manufacturers, spend a great deal of money, time and energy trying to persuade us to throw away our old possessions and buy new ones. Many items and materials are designed to be thrown away, e.g. packaging and newspapers. In this way potentially valuable material is lost and more new energy and resources are used up in the manufacture of replacements and substitutes. So repairing, reusing and recycling materials are integral

aspects of creating a more sustainable society.

__Repair:__ Many products are designed to have a short life span and to be discarded when finished with. Many others which could have a longer life span are similarly discarded when they could have been repaired.

__Reuse:__ This is the best form of recycling because no further energy sources are required. Items can be reused in their unchanged state or used for new purposes.

__Recycle:__ This is the activity by which waste is reprocessed and new items produced for consumption.

Every year we throw away millions of tons of rubbish. A huge proportion of household rubbish is fully recyclable; glass, paper, metal and organic matter, so the amount of waste can be reduced significantly. The success of recycling depends on the commitment of people to separating waste items and to demanding support and leadership from the state, local authorities and industry.

The diagram below outlines some of the benefits of recycling along with the problems associated with waste.

Paper-Plastic-Glass-Oil-Metal-Organic Matter

RECYCLING leads to
1. *Employment*
2. *Conservation of natural resources*
3. *Energy Savings*
4. *Reduction of methane*
5. *A cleaner environment*
6. *Less pollution*

WASTE leads to
1. *Landfill (dump sites)*
2. *Depletion of Resources*
3. *Energy loss*
4. *Methane production*
5. *Litter*
6. *Pollution of land, water, air etc.*

Already in many areas there are bottle banks, waste paper collection depots, acceptance sites for waste oil, scrap yards, also arrangements can be made for the collection of aluminium cans.

As with other issues there must be seen (and heard) to be a demand for it. Letters need to be written, politicians and business people lobbied, and family, friends and neighbours informed.

A New Earth, Gateway Series 2

QUESTIONS

1. Why is the time we are living in referred to as the *Waste Age*?
2. Why does this extract argue in favour of recycling material?

Part Three

Life After Death

CHAPTER EIGHTEEN

THE MYSTERY OF EVIL AND SUFFERING

Introduction

Amongst the many important questions to which the world's religions seek an answer, perhaps the most difficult, is that of *evil* and *suffering*.

Evil and suffering are usually linked together because *evil is wrong and it usually causes suffering*. For example, to explode a bomb in a crowded shopping area is an evil act and it causes terrible suffering to its victims.

Sometimes, when people stop and consider the world around them, they are prompted to ask questions such as:

- *Why is there so much cruelty, illness, suffering and death?*
- *Why do good people suffer while wicked people often seem to do very well for themselves?*

Such questions, raised by the experience of evil and suffering, have caused some people to question the claims some religions, particularly Christianity, make about God. These questions have led some people to wonder if there is really any point in trying to lead a good life.

▲
New York after the events of September 11th

Questions about God

Jews, Christians and Muslims believe that God is:

- *benevolent* – i.e. utterly good and kind;
- *omniscient* – i.e. all-knowing;
- *omnipotent* – i.e. all-powerful.

But some people wonder if this is really so, when they consider the impact of evil and suffering on so many people's lives.

Consider the following objections:

1. If God is so completely good, then God will only want good things to happen.
   Why would a good God allow so much suffering to occur?

2. If God is all-knowing, then God must have known that all this suffering would occur even *before* our world began.
   Why would God create our world while knowing, from the very beginning, that so many people would have to suffer later on?

3. If God is all-powerful, then God can do *anything*.
   Why does God not use this power to prevent or eliminate all suffering in the world?

   It is because there is suffering and evil in the world that some people doubt if God really is good and kind, or whether there is a God at all.

The Nature of Evil

In order to gain some insight into the nature of evil, religious thinkers advise people to make an important distinction between *two* kinds of evil:

- **Moral evil**
  This refers to any action *committed by a human being* that deliberately seeks to inflict harm on another person or thing, e.g. a murder.

- **Non-moral evil**
  This refers to any naturally occurring event, that is *beyond our human power to control or prevent*, which inflicts harm on a person or thing, e.g. an earthquake.

QUESTIONS

1. Why are evil and suffering usually linked together?

2. Give your own example of an evil act and explain you choice.

3. Match the following words in column A with the explanations in column B.

A	B
benevolent	all-knowing
omniscient	all-powerful
omnipotent	utterly good and kind

4. Use the words given in the box to fill in the spaces below.

■ inflict ■ human being ■ beyond ■ murder
■ earthquake ■ control ■ naturally

- Moral evil refers to any action committed by a _____ _____ which deliberately seeks to _____ harm on another person or thing, e.g. _____.

- Non-moral evil refers to any _____ occurring event that is _____ our human power to _____ or prevent which inflicts harm on a person or thing, e.g. an _____.

Moral Evil

Many religious thinkers make a connection between *free will* and the existence of moral evil in our world.

Jews, Christians and Muslims believe that human beings are made in *the image and likeness of God* (see *Genesis* 1:26-27).

In other words, unlike all the other living creatures on earth, humans have been given the *special gift* of free will by God. Only human beings can *choose* to do good or to do evil.

Cain and Abel by
Riminaldi. Cain kills
his brother Abel, see
Genesis 4:1–16.

God wants people to use this gift wisely and well. But God does *not make* people do so.

Some people ask why God did not 'programme' human beings from the very beginning to do only good. But this would reduce humans to little more than *puppets* without free will.

If human beings could do only good things, then they would *not* be free at all.

God gave human beings the gift of free will out of *love*. God wants people to decide for themselves. God offers *guidance* through different religions, but God does *not* seek to control people.

The gift of free will carries with it an awesome responsibility. Sadly, many people make the *wrong* choices. They *abuse* the gift of free will. Their actions cause much suffering.

Moral evil, then, is caused by *human* weakness, greed and negligence. It is *not* God's fault.

QUESTIONS

1. What *special gift* do Jews, Christians and Muslims believe that God has given *only* to human beings?

2. Why did God not simply *programme* human beings from the beginning to do only good?

3. If God does *not* seek to control people, what does God do to *help* them make the right choices?

4. What do the major religions teach is the *cause* of moral evil in our world?

JOURNAL WORK

Read the following extract from the diary of a young Jewish girl named Etty Hillesum. She lived in the Netherlands during the Second World War. At that time, the Nazis were rounding up Jews to transport them to concentration camps, where they would be murdered in gas chambers.

JOURNAL WORK CONTD.

Etty was in hiding. However, she witnessed the brutal treatment of her fellow Jews when they were captured. Deeply troubled, she poured out her heart to God. She wrote:

One thing is becoming increasingly clear to me: that you, God, cannot help us: that we must help you to help ourselves. That is all we can manage these days and also all that matters: that we safeguard that little piece of you, God, in ourselves.

(a) Who did Etty blame for the terrible things that happened to the Jewish people?
(b) Why did she continue to believe in God despite such moral evil?
(c) How did she draw strength from her belief in God?

Non-Moral Evil

Even if we set aside the suffering caused by moral evil, we are still left with the suffering inflicted by non-moral evil, most notably natural disasters.

Religious thinkers argue that such things as earthquakes and volcanic eruptions, for instance, are an unavoidable part of the ordinary workings of nature.

For example, geologists study how the Earth was formed. They tell us that in order for living things to have ever emerged and survived, our planet had to reach, and stay at, just the right point between molten hot and cooled solid.

The crust of our planet has cooled to just the right point where it can and continues to support life. But it is only a crust, i.e. a cooled outer layer. It rests on top of a molten core.

From time to time, this crust moves, cracks and buckles causing earthquakes. When the molten inner core of the planet breaks through the crust, there are volcanic eruptions.

These events are called natural disasters because, tragically, they can cause great harm to many people. But they are an essential part of how the Earth must work if it is to continue to sustain human life on its surface.

It is a sad fact that many people have lost their lives as a result of such natural disasters. But many of these lives *could have been saved*.

- Those in danger could have received advanced warning if the technology had been put in place to detect danger at an early stage.
- Governments could have re-located people away from known earthquake lines, active volcanoes or areas prone to flooding.
- International relief agencies could have been better funded to provide emergency aid to those in need.

All this, however, requires money and the political will to do what is necessary. This has rarely been forthcoming.

QUESTIONS

1. In each case, state whether the following action is (a) a *moral* evil **or** (b) a *non-moral* evil.

   - flooding ■ car theft ■ pick-pocketing ■ storms
   - drought ■ vandalism ■ drunk-driving

2. Religious thinkers claim that natural events such as earthquakes and volcanic eruptions are unfortunately an *essential part* of how the Earth must work if it is to sustain life on its surface. What *reasons* do they have for believing this?

3. (a) State two ways in which human lives could be saved from the effects of natural disasters.
   (b) Why are human lives so often *not* saved in such situations?

JOURNAL WORK

Imagine that you are the director of a famine relief programme in Africa. You are faced with a huge crisis:

- There has been no rain for two years.
- Most of the wells have run dry.
- The harvest has failed.
- There is very little food available.
- The area has been torn apart by a vicious civil war between rival groups who want to control its natural resources. These groups are funded and supplied by powerful people from outside the country.

Over a million people are on the verge of starvation. It is *your* job to organise help for them. You need the help of the richer nations in order to save these people's lives.

Write a letter to the governments of these nations asking for help.
Consider the following issues in your letter:

- law and order;
- food and water;
- transport;
- medical personnel and supplies;
- shelter;
- education for the future.

Also, state what will happen if this help is *not* forthcoming.

WHY DOES GOD NOT DO SOMETHING?

A *miracle* has been defined as:

> *a marvellous or wonderful event which occurs as a result of God's direct action.*

Some people wonder why God does not just work miracles to stop suffering or even prevent it from happening in the first place.

Christians believe that God *does* directly intervene in certain situations. They say that there are well-documented cases where people were cured from diseases that doctors considered incurable and fatal.

Feeding of the Multitude by De Clerch ▼

However, they point out that such cases are *very rare* for good reasons:

- Miracles reveal that God's power is *not* limited by the laws of nature. They give people glimpses of God's greatness and help to strengthen their faith.

- However, miracles must remain the *exception* rather than the rule if God is not to become a puppet-master who controls the world and makes all the decisions for human beings. That would deprive us of our freedom to make choices.

Searching for Answers

We are still left with the suffering caused by both moral and non-moral evil. It raises an important question:

Why would a good and loving God put human beings in a world where suffering and death occur?

In response, Judaism, Christianity and Islam teach that questions about the evil and suffering are beyond our ability to fully answer. Evil is a *mystery*. We may gain insight into the meaning and purpose of evil, but we can never fully understand it.

For example, consider the harm caused by many diseases. Yet, *if there were no diseases, would people appreciate good health*?

This is just one of many perplexing questions. Indeed, the deeper one probes into the mystery of evil, the more complex and perplexing it becomes. So much so that religions such as Christianity, Judaism and Islam teach that, ultimately, only God knows the full reasons for the existence of suffering and evil.

Justice

Religious thinkers claim that the way in which people view life itself has a major role to play in how they understand the meaning and purpose of evil and suffering.

Consider the cases of the Mafia gang lord or the Nazi camp commandant. Both of whom die of old age without ever having to answer for the terrible things they have done in their lives. Or the case of *Jesus of Nazareth*, who was put to death for crimes he did *not* commit.

The Three Crosses
by Rembrandt

If people truly believe that human life begins and *ends* in this world – with no possibility of life after death – then there is no justice to be had. There is little point in enduring evil and suffering.

But if there *is* life after death – where the good are rewarded and the wicked punished – then suffering in this life *has* a meaning and purpose. There *is* justice. Those who endure suffering now will share eternal (i.e. everlasting) joy and peace with God.

Reflection

None of this makes the experience of suffering any easier to undergo. Some people have to cope with terrible tragedies. They suffer greatly.

Religious people draw great strength and encouragement from their belief in God. They do *not* believe that God is remote and uncaring. Christians, for example, believe that *even the Son of God had to suffer*. They also believe that Jesus commanded his followers to respond to suffering by helping those in need. Above all, they believe that they are *not alone*. God is *there* to guide, strengthen and support them through it all.

QUESTIONS

1. Why is the existence of evil and suffering described as a *mystery*?
2. Why does Christianity teach that belief in life after death is important when considering the mystery of evil and suffering?

CHAPTER NINETEEN

REASONS FOR HOPE

Introduction

From earliest times, human beings have believed in some form of life after death. Archaeologists excavating the Shanidar caves in Iraq found evidence that this belief is at least 60,000 years old. They discovered the remains of a child buried in a shallow grave surrounded by flowers. Placing flowers on a grave as an act of remembrance and respect for a person's life is a tradition with very deep roots in human history.

Self-portrait with Death as a Fiddler by Böcklin
▼

Most people are anxious about death, often fearful at the prospect of dying. This is a uniquely *human* concern. Human beings are the *only* creatures on this planet that know they must one day die. We know that all things in the universe, from stars to snowdrops, have a certain, limited lifespan. Death is an *inescapable fact*.

The Meaning of Death

We may define *death* as

> the permanent ending of all the bodily functions that keep a person alive.

The word *dying* refers to the *way* in which a person's life comes to an end.

How can one know if a person is dead as distinct from being in a *coma*? This is an important question. Consider the situation where a person has offered to donate his/her vital organs for transplant surgery upon his/her death. The doctors must be *certain* the person is dead before their removal. The World Health Organisation provided guidelines for doctors on this matter in 1968.

Doctors diagnose someone as being in a *coma* when it has been determined that:

- The person is in a state of deep unconsciousness from which he/she cannot be awakened.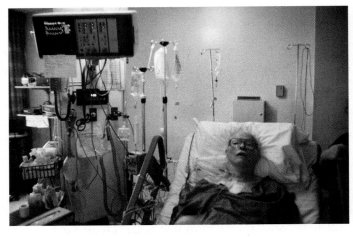
- He/she does not respond to painful stimuli.
- The person's brain, however, *continues* to control the vital functions of his/her body, i.e. breathing and heartbeat.

A person is pronounced *dead* when it has been established that:

- His/her brain has *ceased* to control the vital functions of his/her body.
- There is no evidence of muscular activity or blood pressure.
- He/she is unable to breathe without the aid of a life-support machine.

QUESTIONS

1. What is the meaning of the tradition of placing flowers on a person's grave?
2. Why is it said that death is an *uniquely human concern*?
3. What is *death*?
4. Use the words in the box below to fill in the missing words below.

■ unaided ■ pressure ■ vital ■ unable ■ ceased ■ no

A person is pronounced dead when it has been established that:

- His/her brain has _____ to control the _____ functions of his/her body.
- There is _____ evidence of activity or blood _____.
- He/she is _____ to breathe _____ by a machine.

Attitudes to Death

Thanks to improvements in public health and diet, most people today in the developed world can look forward to reaching at least seventy years of age. Women, on average, enjoy a longer lifespan than men.

Yet, sociologists have noticed that hand in hand with this improvement in life expectancy, there has been a considerable change in public attitudes towards death. Fewer people are willing to discuss the subject openly. It seems that, for many people in Western society, death has become *too distant* and *unreal*. Something they would rather ignore.

Consider the following:

■ Those people who continue to smoke cigarettes despite evidence that they are exposing themselves to a high risk of lung cancer.

■ Every year hundreds of people die in traffic accidents. Yet, some people persist in driving in a reckless fashion placing both their own lives and those of other people at risk.

■ The indifference with which some people view important issues such as abortion, poverty or the environment.

Sooner or later, however, every person *must* face the reality of death. Most often, this is caused by the death of a close family member or a good friend. If the person dies young, people are shocked and say,

> *It simply doesn't make sense! How can an accident or disease cause the death of someone I love?*

And even if the person was elderly and died peacefully, people often say,

> *Only the body has died; it was just worn out. Surely that can't be the end. Will I never see this person again?*

Although it can be very hard to see it at the time, facing up to the reality of death can be a *positive* experience. It can lead one to re-evaluate one's whole life and the direction it should take.

Consider the following story:

Alfred Nobel
▼

> *One morning Alfred Nobel awoke to read his own obituary. The obituary was printed as a result of a simple journalistic error ... Any man would be disturbed under the circumstances, but to Alfred Nobel the shock was overwhelming. He saw himself as the world saw him – 'the dynamite king', the great industrialist ... None of his true intentions – the breakdown of barriers that*

separated people and ideas – were recognised or given consideration. As he read his obituary with horror, Nobel resolved to make clear to the world the true meaning and purpose of his life. His last will and testament would be the expression of his life's ideals ... The result was the most valued of prizes given to those who had done the most for the cause of world peace — the Nobel Peace Prize.

N. Halasz, *Nobel*

QUESTIONS

1. What impact do you think cinema and television violence have had on making death seem distant and unreal for some people? Explain your answer.

2. Read the story of Alfred Nobel one more. Then answer the following questions:

   (a) Why was Nobel shocked when he read his own obituary?

   (b) How had he wanted people to remember him?

   (c) What was his lasting reaction to this strange experience?

The Source of Hope

Humanists say that God does *not* exist. They believe that life in this world is all that there is and that death marks the final end for each person. In this view, human suffering and death which each person must face and accept can only be considered as a brutal fact.

Christians believe that God *does* exist. God is utterly good and loving. It would be *completely out of character* for God to give people life, to encourage them to live good lives and then, one day, to simply annihilate them.

The Human Person

Consider what it *means* to be a human being.

Humans are *unique*. Of all the creatures that inhabit the Earth, only humans are capable of imagining, choosing, planning, loving and worshipping. The source of these unique capacities in each human being is called the *soul*.

The Catholic Church's teaching on the soul states that:

■ Each person is *one being*, composed of a body and a soul.

- The body is the visible, *physical* aspect of the person and the soul is the invisible, *spiritual* aspect of the person.
- The soul *gives life* to the body.
- The soul is the constant, unchanging *core* of each individual man and woman's personality as they go through life.

Consider what one Christian psychologist has to say to illustrate this point.

> *In spite of the passage of years, in spite of change and development, I am the 'I' of twenty or thirty years ago. So many things have happened, travel, thought, adventure, the many daily experiences. Nevertheless, I am myself, I have retained my identity. My body has changed, my mind grown, but the soul by which I am what I am, abides.*
> Adapted from Prof. Peter Dempsey, *Psychology for All*

▲ From conception to old age.

Some religions, most notably Hinduism, teach that the body is the prison of the soul. Christians do *not* share this view.

Christians worship Jesus, who is *God-made-flesh*. The body is *as much* a gift from God as is the soul. The soul *needs* the body, as it is through our bodies that we are able:

- to recognise other people and be recognised by them;
  and
- to express ourselves and communicate with one another.

Body and soul *belong together*. Together they give each person his/her own unique identity. This is why Christians believe in *the resurrection of the body* (see either The Apostles' Creed or the Nicene Creed).

Resurrection

Christians trust in the promise of Jesus that they too will experience their own personal resurrection from the dead. They believe that the relationship they have formed with God in this life will *continue* after death.

Catholics believe that the soul is *immortal*, i.e. it does not die when separated from the body at death.

Whereas Hinduism teaches that the ultimate aim of life is for the soul to forever cast off the body, Catholicism takes a very *different* view. Catholics believe that the soul will be *re-united* with the body at the end of time.

The risen Jesus shows what will happen to everyone. Like Jesus, people will *not* merely be restored to their old lives, rather they will all be *transformed* to live a new kind of life.

This *resurrected* life will be one *beyond* all the limitations of life in this world. Death will have *no power* over us whatsoever.

Just as the risen Jesus was still recognisably the *same* person the apostles had known *before* his death, so too will each person survive death with his/her individual identity *intact*.

Death is *not* the end. It should be seen as an *entry* to a new kind of life to which all people are invited – *eternal life with God*.

▲ *The Resurrection; the Angels Rolling Away the Stone* by Blake

QUESTIONS

1. Explain the humanist view of death.
2. What is the Christian response to the humanist view of death?
3. (a) Which religion teaches that the body is *the prison of the soul*?
    (b) Do Catholics agree with this view? Why?
4. What does it mean to say that the human soul is *immortal*?

CHAPTER TWENTY

THE PROMISE OF ETERNAL LIFE

The Meaning of Eternity

High up in the North in the land called Svithjod, there stands a rock. It is a hundred miles high and a hundred miles wide. Once every thousand years a little bird comes to this rock to sharpen its beak. When the rock, has thus been worn away, then a single day of eternity will have gone by.

This old Scandinavian legend imagines eternity as if it were the same as earthly time but just went on and on forever without end. This is *not* the Christian idea of eternity.

Christians believe that a clue as to what eternity is like can be found in the Bible.

In the *Old Testament* account of when God appeared to Moses in the form of a burning bush, God told Moses that his name is '*I am*' (see *Exodus* 3:14). This means that God lives, knows and acts always in the present tense. For God there is no past or future, *only now*. The *life everlasting* that Christians pray for in the Apostles' Creed is

Moses Before the Burning Bush by Raphael

not a reality with a past or a future but only a present – *an everlasting now.*

However, because this world is dominated by the passage of time, where people's lives are ruled by the ticking of the clock, there will always be great difficulty in trying to imagine what eternity will be like. Human language is designed to describe *this* world and it is of limited value when trying to describe things that go beyond our human experience. The best one can do is try to draw analogies as to what heaven and hell will be like, based on one's experience of goodness and wickedness respectively in *this* world. But they are only intended to act as helpful images and *not* to be taken literally.

Further, it is important to remember that one should *not* regard heaven and hell as physical realities. Here is a story that illustrates how earthbound some people's thinking can be.

A foreign diplomat once mentioned the word 'heaven' in a conversation with the Communist leader Nikita Khrushchev. The latter gave the diplomat a look of disgust and remarked: *'For goodness sake, don't talk about heaven. We sent astronauts up into space and they couldn't find any trace of it!'*

Khrushchev failed to understand that heaven and hell are *not* physical places above and below the Earth. They are *spiritual* realities.

> *We are not talking about places so much as experiences, experiences of total love or of its complete absence. Anyone who has known the joy of being in love or the anguish of a broken heart knows that the images we use only serve to give an idea of the experience. This is truer when we come to talk about union with, or separation from, God.*
>
> Sean Goan, *The Word*

QUESTIONS

1. Why do human beings have great difficulty in trying to explain what eternity is like?
2. What point did Khrushchev fail to understand when criticising the Christian belief in heaven?

Judgment

Christians believe that human life is divided into two phases:

- life *before* death *and*   - life *after* death.

Death does not mark the final end of each person. Rather, death is the moment of *transition* (i.e. crossing over) from this life to the next.

After death, each person will be *judged* (i.e. held accountable) for his/her behaviour in this life according to the standards Jesus set. Read the following extract.

When the Son of Man comes in glory, all the nations will be assembled before him and he will separate people one from another as the shepherd separates sheep from goats. He will place the sheep on his right hand and the goats on his left.

Then the Lord will say to those on his right hand, 'Come, you whom my father has blessed, take for your heritage the kingdom prepared for you since the foundation of the world. For I was hungry and you gave me food; I was thirsty and you gave me drink; I was a stranger and you made me welcome; naked and you clothed me, sick and you visited me, in prison and you came to see me.'

The Last Judgement by Michelangelo
▼

> *Then the virtuous will say to him in reply, 'Lord, when did we see you hungry and feed you; or thirsty and give you drink? When did we see you a stranger and make you welcome; naked and clothe you; sick or in prison and go to see you?'*
>
> *And the Lord will answer, 'I tell you solemnly, in so far as you did this to one of the least of these brothers and sisters of mine, you did it to me.'*
>
> *Next he will say to those on his left hand, 'Go away from me. For I was hungry and you never gave me food; I was thirsty and you never gave me anything to drink; I was a stranger and you never made me welcome, naked and you never clothed me, sick and in prison and you never visited me.'*
>
> *Then it will be their turn to ask, 'Lord, when did we see you hungry or thirsty, a stranger or naked, sick or in prison, and did not come to your help?'*
>
> *Then he will answer, 'I tell you solemnly, in so far as you neglected to do this to one of the least of these, you neglected to do it to me.'*
>
> *And they will go away to eternal punishment, and the virtuous to eternal life.*
> *Matthew 25:31-46*

If people cannot see God in the people they meet in *this* life, how can they expect to see God in the *next*?

In this life, however, it is never too late to repent and to seek God's forgiveness. Consider the story of the *good thief* who was crucified alongside Jesus.

> *One of the criminals hanging there mocked him. 'Are you not the Christ?' he said. 'Save yourself and us as well.' But the other spoke up and rebuked him. 'Have you no fear of God at all?' he said. 'We got the same sentence as he did, but in our case we deserved it: we are paying for what we did. But this man has done nothing wrong.' 'Jesus,' he said 'remember me when you come into your kingdom.' 'Indeed, I promise you,' Jesus replied 'today you will be with me in paradise.'*
> *Luke 23:39-43*

God is always there, waiting for people to turn towards him. God does not force people to behave in certain ways. God gives people the *freedom* to choose how to live their lives. By their moral choices in *this* life, people decide their own fate in the *next* life.

QUESTIONS

1. What does it mean to say that people will be *judged* after death?
2. What is the central message of the story of the *good thief*?
3. Why do Christians think it is important to make good moral choices in this life?

Hell

Jesus often spoke of *Gehenna*, meaning the unquenchable fire. The Catholic Church follows Jesus' teaching that *hell* exists.

Many people today have difficulty with the whole idea of hell, i.e. an eternity of punishment. They find it hard to reconcile hell with belief in an utterly good and loving God. However, Paul taught the early Christians that:

▲
The Dammed by
Michelangelo

> *God wants everyone to be saved.*
> *1 Timothy 2:4*

Yet, this is beyond even the power of God. Why?

The answer to this question is that *God respects human freedom*. God is *not* cruel. God has given human beings the power to choose between good and evil.

Human beings effectively pass judgment upon *themselves* by the way they live their lives in this world.

Consider the following story:

> *An architect, who had worked for a large company for many years, and who was soon to retire, was called in one day by the board of directors and given plans for a fine house to be built in the best quarter of town. The chairman instructed him to spare no expense, using the finest materials and best builders. As the house began to go up, the architect began to think, 'Why use such costly materials?' so he began to use poor materials and to hire poor quality workmen, and he put the difference in the cost into his own pocket. When the house was finished, it looked very fine on the outside, but it certainly would not last long.*
>
> *Shortly after it was finished, the board of directors held another meeting to which the architect was called. The chairman made a speech, thanking the architect for his long service to the company, as a reward for which they were making him a retirement present of the house!*

If a person *freely* and *knowingly* pursues his/her selfish desires by indulging in a destructive lifestyle, rejecting any involvement in making this world a better place, choosing to cut him/herself off from God and other people, then they have *chosen* the alternative to heaven.

QUESTIONS

1. Why is it beyond even the power of God for *everyone to be saved*?
2. Read the story of the architect once more. Use this story to explain Christian belief about hell.

JOURNAL WORK

Christians today do not believe hell to be a physical place 'full of fire and burning sulphur', but they do believe hell to really exist and that the experience of evil in this world can give some idea as to what hell is like.
Colm Kilcoyne writes:

> *When I let what is dark and jealous in me control me. When a home is controlled by brutality. When money is short. When life has taught us to hate who we are. Hell on earth is the experience of life unravelling, of the crushing of what is beautiful in us. The other hell is that for eternity.*

In which life experiences do you catch a glimpse of hell? Explain you answer.

Purgatory

The word *purgatory* is not to be found in the Bible. However, the idea of purgatory can be traced back to the *Old Testament* (see *Second Maccabees* 12:45).

Catholics believe that purgatory is required to prepare those people who are not yet ready to enjoy the *Beatific Vision* (i.e. to enter God's presence). Purgatory is a process of *purification*, where a person roots out or *purges* all those things that prevent him/her from completely loving God and other people.

Some people, however, may have *already* done their purgatory in *this* world through their suffering. Others may not. There may be all kinds of barriers in their lives that obstruct their entry into heaven.

As with any experience that helps a person to grow in genuine love it involves pain, but not of a physical kind. The pain of purgatory will be the realisation of how far short one has fallen from loving God and one's neighbour, coupled with a great desire to enter heaven. Once people have allowed God's love to purge those things from their lives, which prevent them from loving others as they should, God will draw them to share eternal life in heaven.

N.B.
There is no way of knowing how long a person must remain in purgatory. The afterlife does not measure time in the same way as this world. It is beyond our ability to know the answer.

QUESTIONS

1. What does it mean to enjoy the *Beatific Vision*?
2. What do Catholics believe about purgatory?

Heaven

In our twenty-first-century culture, the word heaven conjures up many misleading images – clouds, winged people playing harps and so on. Indeed, the playwright George Bernard Shaw once remarked that people had made heaven sound so *dull* that no one with a bit of life in him/her would want to go there.

We need to disregard these popular but *misleading* images of heaven, as they can distract us from developing an accurate, if only limited, understanding of what Christians mean by *heaven*.

When speaking of heaven, people must keep in mind the limitations of human language. As the poet John Donne wrote:

The Resurrection
▼

The tongues of angels, the tongues of glorified saints shall not be able to express what heaven is.

Christians believe that those people who have tried with all their heart to love God and their fellow human beings, will be brought immediately after death into the presence of God. They will experience the community of perfect love that is heaven.

Heaven is the complete answer to our deepest human longings. There all our worries will be removed, our needs met and our hopes fulfilled. People will enjoy perfect happiness and peace in the presence of God.

This is very difficult for people to grasp here and now, for as Paul wrote:

No eye has seen, nor ear has heard, nor the heart of man nor woman conceived what God has prepared for those who love him.
1 Corinthians 2:9

QUESTIONS

1. Whom do Christians believe will be brought immediately after death into the presence of God?
2. In which experiences of life in *this* world do people catch a glimpse of what heaven is like?
3. Read the following story from China. It explores the difference between heaven and hell.

A long time ago in a place far away, a small group of people were being led on a tour by a messenger from God.

As they travelled down a long corridor, the messenger opened the first door and told them, 'This is heaven'.

They looked inside and saw a huge banquet table full of delicious foods. All the men and women who sat around the table looked healthy and well fed. And the room was filled with joyful noises. In the hands of all the people were four-foot-long forks that they used to feed one another. Then, the messenger led them to a second door and said, 'And this is hell'.

The door opened. Inside was another huge banquet table filled to overflowing with all sorts of delicious foods. But all the men and women who sat around the table looked horribly gaunt and emaciated. Whining, groaning, and angry shouts filled the room. Again, each of the people held a four-foot-long fork; but this time each of them was trying to feed himself or herself.

QUESTIONS CONTD.

Christians believe that the kind of person one is or has become at the time of death is the kind of person one *continues to be* in the next life.

How does this story explain the *difference* between those who are in heaven and those who are in hell?

Concluding Remarks

When someone dies, those who are left behind don't stop loving him/her. Human love refuses to accept division by death. Christians believe that this is all the more true in the case of God's love.

God wishes to share eternal life with all people. This is the *destiny* God offers each of us. It is an *invitation*, not a command. Human beings, by their moral decisions, choose their eternal destiny. Yet, even if they have spent their entire lives turned away from God, God is ready to forgive, even in the final moments of a person's life. God's love has no limits, it is forever. As Paul writes:

> *I am convinced that there is nothing in death or life – nothing in all creation that can separate us from the love of God in Christ Jesus Our Lord.*
> Romans 8:38-39

A Final Prayer

After reflecting on the ups and downs of his life, a leading Catholic clergyman, John Henry Newman, wrote the following prayer.

All below heaven changes:
spring,
summer,
autumn,
each has its turn.

The fortunes of the world change;
what was high, lies low;
what was low, lies high.
Riches take wing and flee;
bereavements happen.
Friends become enemies,
and enemies become friends.
Our wishes, aims and plans change.

There is nothing stable,
but you, O my God!
And you are the centre and life of all
who change,
who trust you as their Father,
who look to you
and are content to put themselves
into you hands.

(Apologia Pro Vita Sua)

This is what faith is all about.

KUWAIT
A NEW BEGINNING

by Gail Seery

MOTIVATE
PUBLISHING

Published by
Motivate Publishing

PO Box 2331
Dubai, UAE
Tel: (04) 824060
Fax: (04) 824436

PO Box 43072
Abu Dhabi, UAE
Tel: (02) 311666
Fax: (02) 311888

London House
26/40, Kensington High Street
London W8 4PF
Tel: (071) 938 2222
Fax: (071) 937 7293

Directors:
Obaid Humaid Al Tayer
Ian Fairservice

First published 1993

© 1993 Gail Seery and
Motivate Publishing

ISBN 1 873544 40 5

Printed by Emirates Printing Press, Dubai

British Library Cataloguing-in-Publication Data.
A catalogue record for this book is available
from the British Library.